MY LIFE IN PORN:

The Bobby Blake Story

MY LIFE IN PORN

THE BOBBY BLAKE STORY

by BOBBY BLAKE with JOHN R. GORDON

Running Press
PHILADELPHIA · LONDON

Notice: Names have been changed throughout to protect the privacy of those close to the author. These are indicated by single quotes (") when they first appear.

9 8 7 6 5 4 3 2 1

Library of Congress Cataloging-in-Publication Number 2007943025
ISBN 978-0-78672-096-5

Edited by Don Weise
Typography: Garamond and Agency

Running Press Book Publishers
2300 Chestnut Street
Philadelphia, PA 19103-4371

Visit us on the web!
www.runningpress.com

TABLE OF CONTENTS

PREFACE

YOU CAN'T DEAL WITH PEOPLE IF YOU'VE NEVER WALKED IN THEIR SHOES

With the life I've led you might be surprised to learn that I'm a keen student of the Bible. But I am, and have been ever since I first learned to read as a child. The Bible story that speaks most strongly to my life is the Tale of the Prodigal Son: in fact, 'Prodigal Son' is one of the titles I considered for this book. As you will recall, the prodigal son leaves the family home and goes out into the world, defying his father's wishes because he is eager for worldly experiences. And he goes off and he has those experiences. To start off with he's enjoying them, but after a time he realizes that the world out there is harsh and heartless, and eventually, defeated and starving, he makes his way back home. He arrives at his father's door expecting nothing but rejection, but instead his father, rejoicing that his sinning son has repented of his misdeeds, kills a fatted calf to celebrate his return.

The good son, the one who stays home and has nothing to repent for, is mad at the father for that, but that's a whole other story.

The Tale of the Prodigal Son is one that is often seen in negative terms of a particular sort: the defiant young man's experiences out in the world are seen as regrettable mistakes, things he shouldn't have done which have brought him low. A lot of people would say that he would be a better person if he had been like the good son and stayed home and done his duty, and the conventional focus of the tale is on the prodigal son's regret and repentance for his reckless actions. But the tale speaks to me in a somewhat different way, because although I do have regrets. I don't believe that God makes mistakes, by which I mean that God intended for the prodigal son to have the experiences he had. Those experiences were neither punishment nor were they errors: they were lessons in reality. And God intended that the prodigal son would one day be able to use what he learned from those experiences for some good purpose.

For a porn star to talk in terms of the Bible may seem unusual, even profane, but like many African-Americans, particularly those in the South, I was brought up in the church, so it's my frame of reference as well as my moral and spiritual guide. In any case, right from the start I was deeply serious about my religious beliefs, and my commitment only grew stronger as the years went by, to the point where, at age nineteen, I followed my vocation and became, for a time, a minister of the church.

Had I continued along that path it's quite possible that I

might now be an ordained pastor leading a large congreg-ation, and be known as a preacher rather than a porn star. The Bobby Blake you know would never have existed. But it turned out that God had other plans for me.

There came a time in my life when, like the Prodigal Son, I had to leave the church and the place of my birth and go out there in the far country. I had to get away from every-thing I had grown up with as a child in order to grow up as a man. I had to learn about myself and about other people in a different context from the one I was familiar with. And that was my sojourn in the world of pornography, which is the subject of much of this book.

It was during that time that I worked as an erotic dancer, an escort, a model, and a performer in adult films. It was then that I became Bobby Blake the Porn Star, and it's most likely because you've seen some of the films I made as Bobby Blake that you're reading this book. It was an intense, amaz-ing, and often highly enjoyable period of my life, and I am not ashamed of it. Now, looking back on it, I do regret it. I do wish that I had had some other life. But I'm not ashamed of it.

Paradoxical as it will sound, in all the years I was working in the adult entertainment business I never turned my back on God or the Bible teachings I had grown up with. I never forgot where I had come from, and when I felt the pull I returned to the church of my youth, to the town of my birth, and now I live in the very same house I grew up in, and I toil in God's house, and I strive to do good works.

My experiences in the porn business have left me more

humble, more understanding of human frailty, and more able to help others than I would ever have been otherwise. Above all I feel I have something to offer those struggling with their sexuality. Young men contemplating suicide because their church leaders are telling them that being gay means they will go to hell. Men who prefer men sexually but marry out of a need for societal approval, whether they be pastors or church elders, bishops or regular folks. Men who marry to please their parents while never for one moment truly loving their wives. All these men know they can talk to me, and because of the experiences I have been through they know I won't judge them. They know I'll understand.

My main role in the church I attend now is that of counselor, and you would be surprised how often, even in our seemingly tolerant times, I get emails and phone calls from people saying to me, "Bobby, you saved my life." When someone tells me that he was going to give up, give in and end his life, but through speaking to me he's been inspired to carry on and find his own truth instead, I understand why I had to take the route in my life that I took. I understand that God had a plan for me, and that, curiously enough, it took me into the world of adult entertainment, and then it took me out again so I might help other suffering souls.

A lot of people out there will disapprove of many of the choices I've made in my life, but I don't apologize for it. There's an old song in the African-American church, and there's a saying that echoes it that runs, "Once you have given the best of your services, if men don't understand you, God will understand and say well done." And that is what I have always tried to do in my life, in whatever capacity I am acting: give the best of my services. For that reason I don't look for the outside world to approve my perspective or my views. In fact, it seems to me that's what's wrong with many of us today: as gay people we want the larger community to accept our views and to endorse our agendas. I'm not looking for that: it's not what's important to me. What I'm looking for, and what I maintain to this day, is a close relationship with my Father, in the sure belief that He will understand and that, when my time on Earth is through, He will say to me, "Because you've given the best of your service, well done."

Other people will ask, "Well, if you had all this religion, if you had all these family values, if you had all of this Christian righteousness inside you, how in the world could you leave the church and the ministry and perform in hardcore gay and bisexual pornography?"

Although that is not all that this book is about, I hope that what follows will answer that question as far as it can be answered, as far as any man's reasons and motives can be explained and understood.

—Bobby Blake

ACKNOWLEDGMENTS

I would like to thank my parents for the love they have shared with me down through the years. They have always been in my corner in everything I do: to stop me when I am wrong and praise me when I am right. Thank you for even today doing things for me that are not required for you to do: I love you with all my heart. If I could give you the world I would do so. To my sister: I love you with all my heart: thanks for being the best sister a brother could have. Remember how I used to bring my dates to the house and you would look them over and say "yes" or "no"? How you would even say, "He fine," or, "He got it going on!" and give me the green light. . . .

Thanks to Mrs. Gwen Clemons for making me write my story: it's because of you this book got written. Thanks for the love, and for being a friend through all my ups and downs.

Mrs. Abe W. Reed: Thanks for being a true friend who's never been afraid to tell me when I'm right and when I'm wrong. You have always stood by me and for that I love you and want to say thanks. Thank you for all the home-cooked meals!

To my two sons, Davin Clemons and Darnell Gooch Jr., for being in my life: the both of you have been a guiding light. Thank you for inspiring me to go back to college and get my degree and go on to work on my master's degree: you have been there for me through every dark night. You told me to hold on. Thanks for checking on me all the time, saying, "Go to bed, get your rest; we'll do it for you." I love the both of you with all my body, mind, and soul.

Producer Edward James: Thanks from my heart for showing me the ropes. You made me the business-minded person I am. There would never have been a Bobby Blake if not for you. Thank you for always being there: even today you are always there for me.

And last but not least, thank you to Patrik-Ian Polk for putting me in touch with Johnny Gordon, my co-writer on this book.

CHAPTER ONE:

A TOUGH START

I was born in Memphis, Tennessee on August 11th, 1957. A Leo. I was seriously premature. On top of that I had numerous health complications. I had to have an emergency blood transfusion shortly after I was born or else I would have died on the same day that I came into the world. My traumatized mother was told that I would most likely die anyway, despite the transfusion and the best efforts of the medical staff. That anxiety hardened into certainty in her distraught mind, torturing her as the weeks went by and my health failed to improve. As it turned out I didn't die, but I was in that hospital for over a year. Recently I saw my medical records, and in with them was a photograph of myself as a new-born baby. I was amazed to see how tiny and frail I looked, a little bitty something with tubes going in and out of me, about as big as a finger, just so vulnerable. When I look at the huge, muscular bodybuilder I've become today, this strong physical specimen who is lusted after by so many men and women, I'm amazed at how things can shift around.

My mother, who was always mentally fragile, had had one nervous breakdown while she was carrying me. After I was born, her belief that I was going to die caused her to have a second breakdown. My father had deserted her during her pregnancy, and although I have every reason to believe that she loved me and wanted me with her, she was simply unable to cope with caring for a sickly newborn baby. Indeed at that time she was unable to even care for herself, and as a result of her deteriorating mental state she was eventually institutionalized. As a consequence of that, and because my biological father had no interest in caring for or raising me, I was placed in a foster-home by the State of Tennessee directly upon leaving the hospital. So I can't say that to start off with I ever knew my biological mother at all.

My foster-mother was an older lady in her very early seventies who saw it as her Christian duty to help children in need of a safe, decent, and loving environment. I never knew her husband, as he passed when I was very young. My foster-mother raised me, and another boy who she was also fostering, on her own. His name was Bobby. He was several years older than me, and was always very protective towards me, and it was from him that I took the first part of my name when I went into adult films.

My foster-mother also had a biological daughter, but this daughter was already in her forties when I was a baby and so, unsurprisingly, didn't live with us. Despite that I considered her my foster-sister. My foster-sister had a son who was already a grown man when I was born, so I found myself in the unusual situation of being foster-uncle to a nephew who was older than I was.

My foster-mother was very loving, but also very religious and very strict. She taught me and Bobby to say "yes, sir" and "no, sir" and "yes, ma'am" and "no, ma'am," and be respectful to our elders and obedient. If we weren't obedient we'd get a whipping. We were expected to do yard-work and chores around the house to earn money for treats for ourselves—trips to theme-parks and, the like—so from a very early age I was taught the value of money and the importance of hard work. Sometimes Bobby and I would even go out and sweep the streets round about the local area to earn quarters from neighbors. My foster-mother cooked every day from fresh ingredients, so we always had good balanced meals and we never ate fast food, which is, I believe, why I am so healthy today.

She was a medium-height lady, very nice-looking, and she would dress up smart and wear big hats to church. She prayed a lot, and was very God-fearing. She would take me on a regular basis to church services, to Sunday school and Bible class. She and another lady who was an assistant minister in the church we attended would take me on trips to visit other churches round about Memphis as well. Tennessee is in the heart of the Bible Belt, and Memphis is considered the Holy Land of the United States because it's a center for four major denominations: CME (Christian Methodist Episcopal), AME (African Methodist Episcopal), AME-Zion, and The Church of God in Christ, so I got exposure to different styles of worship from an early age. However, although I visited all kinds of churches at this time, we ourselves were devout Methodists.

Later on, through the influence of 'Lou', my first serious romantic partner, I left my home church and joined his, becoming for a time a Baptist, and even going so far as to become an assistant minister in the Baptist church. But it didn't take me long to realize that I prefer the more formal, hierarchical way the Methodist church is run, and so it was to Methodism I returned after my sojourn in the world of pornography.

Despite her age, for the first eight years of my life I believed that my foster-mother was my real mother, and during that time I had no contact with my biological mother and no knowledge of her existence. At age eight my foster-mother sat me down and told me that I wasn't really her child, and that I had a real mother somewhere who had been unable to care for me on account of having mental health problems. It was profoundly disturbing to my eight-year-old self to hear that since my foster-mother had always loved me as her own, and now here she was telling me that I had another mother who was somehow my real mother even though I had never met her or known her. I found it very hard to hear. It was devastating, but I had no choice but to deal with it. And of course it helped that I never doubted the reality of my foster-mother's love for me.

When I was with my foster-mother we lived in an area of Memphis called Orange Mound. Orange Mound was the first African-American neighborhood in the United States to be actually built by African-Americans, on land bought from former plantation owners. It was founded in 1890 and by 1900 it was famous enough to be billed as "the largest concentration of blacks in the U.S. outside of Harlem," and was a vibrant, exciting, and affirming place to be. Although it declined during the desegregation period because younger residents began to move away, in recent years it has been revitalized, and throughout its entire history 90% of Orange Mound's African-American residents have always owned their own homes. So even though it's not the wealthiest area of Memphis there's a lot of pride there, and a lot of history of African-American independent-mindedness, and it's where I live today.

My foster-mother's house was over a hundred years old. The floors were all the original hardwood from when it was first built, and it had two fireplaces and an old stove in the kitchen. There was marble in the bathroom, the rooms were spacious, and the ceilings high. All the furniture was cherry wood. There were porches front and back, and in the yard was a great old oak tree. It was said that my grandmother's father planted that tree for her when she was a little girl, so my foster-mother's family had been in that house for a long time, almost since it was first built.

I never rebelled against my foster-mother's religious strictures or her rules. I was an obedient, pious child who studied hard and did my chores round the house and yard work. Even so I still received the occasional whipping, as when a cousin and I got caught stealing tomatoes from his grandmother's garden. His grandmother whipped us. When she was told about it his mother whipped us, his father whipped us, and when my foster-mother heard about what I'd done she whipped me, too. So I ended up getting four whippings over three tomatoes. I can't say it's a memory I look back on with any fondness, but today I'm grateful for the discipline my foster-mother instilled in me from a very early age.

Is whipping discipline or bullying?

Whippings or not, I loved my foster-mother very much, and she loved me as much as any real mother could. On her deathbed—she died at the age of eighty-six—she asked her grandson to take care of me and make sure I always had everything I needed. He took her dying request to heart, and he and his wife at once offered to legally adopt me. I was then fifteen years old, and it was an offer I was proud and delighted to accept. And so I switched from being my foster-mother's grandson's uncle to being his son and, since my foster-mother had passed and I was too young to live on my own, I went to live with him and his wife on the other side of the city. Many years later my adoptive father allowed me to buy my foster-mother's home from him, and that's how come I'm still living in Orange Mound, in the house I grew up in, to this day.

But all that lay ahead. In the meantime life was good, and I was a happy child growing up in an orderly, respectable home, who knew he was loved. Then at the age of ten my real mother reappeared in my life, and my world was turned upside-down.

CHAPTER TWO:

BLOOD KIN

My foster-mother was always completely supportive of my involvement with my blood family; she understood how important it was for me to know and have contact with my real mother and my real brother and sister. But it surely must have been painful and difficult for her when she was informed that my mother had been through the courts to establish that, since she was well again, she was now fit to care for her children, and that she wanted me back. My foster-mother kept whatever pain she was feeling from me, however, and we stayed in touch by telephone throughout the entire time I was living with my real mother. We talked regularly, and she continued to let me know that she loved me and wanted what was best for me.

My real mother visited me at my foster-mother's home several times before she took me away, so we got to know each other a little before I went to live with her. There was no build-up to her first visit: she arrived at the house one day and my foster-mother introduced me to her and told me,

"Bobby, this is your mother." And there she was, standing in front of me—a beautiful black lady, very smartly-dressed, very together-looking, with no hint in her manner of the mental problems she had had to deal with in the past. She told me that I had a brother and sister who had also been fostered, and that we were all going to live together as a family.

It's hard now to remember what I felt at that time. Most likely I didn't really want to leave my foster-mother's home, but she took pains to make the transition to my biological mother's care feel as natural as possible, an act of great unselfishness on her part. And my real mother did want me: she wanted me enough to come for me, and maybe any child who learns he's been fostered or adopted longs for that, to be claimed by his biological parent.

My mother moved me and my brother and sister into a pleasant, spacious three-bedroom house she was renting in a middle-class black area of South Memphis called Westwood. She was working two jobs at the same time to support us. After so many years I forget what her second job was, but her main job was working as a nurse's assistant at a Jewish hospital. She was mentally strong to start off with, working every hour there was, and determined that she was going to make our family work. It was strange and a little bit scary to suddenly find myself living with three other people who, though they were my blood kin, I simply didn't know.

My real brother, 'Daniel,' was four years older than me, my real sister 'May' two years older. They had been fostered together, by the same family, and at the time they seemed close to each other in a way I felt they would never be close to me, though events during the time we were living with our mom were to drive a serious and permanent wedge between them.

My foster-mother had always forbidden me to go to North Memphis on the grounds that it was a bad area, rough and crime-ridden, the sort of place where the people fight the police in the streets, deal drugs and, as she would put it, "get in a whole mess of trouble." North Memphis was where my first serious romantic partner was from, and it was also the area my brother and sister were brought up in, and my foster-mother was right about it. My two siblings had been brought up very differently from me: they were not reared in the church, and from a young age Daniel was in trouble with the law and May was boy-crazy.

Daniel was wild even before he came to live with us. When he was at his foster-home he was already using drugs and getting involved with petty crime. He could also be extremely violent. One day he came home and the family was all frying fish. He asked them could he have some of the fish and they told him no, which turned out to be a big mistake because he took all that fish and he dumped it straight into the garbage. And he said, "If I ain't gon' eat, then nobody's gon' eat." And no one said or did a thing, because another time he had run them all out of the house with a butcher knife, and the only thing that had stopped him from doing something really crazy was his foster-mother pulling a gun on him. So Daniel was wild.

Even today my brother can be real violent. He's slowed down a little, but it's still in him. About five years ago I went

to visit him in a hospital—he was in for a minor operation—
and he asked me to buy him some cigarettes. Fine. I don't
smoke myself, never have, but I don't judge, so I did it. The
next day I went to visit him a second time and he asked me
to get him another carton of cigarettes. When I told him no,
I wasn't gon' do that, he went crazy: he ripped the needle out
his arm and started tearing up the hospital room in a rage. A
few moments later security came crashing in and forcibly
restrained him. Eventually they got him settled down, a
nurse put the drip back in his arm, and I said to him, "Are
you done?" He didn't say anything, just kinda looked at me.
So I told him, "You know you're only hurting yourself." And
I left it right there because there was nothing else to be said.
Despite his violence I've never been afraid of my brother, and
even today I love him. But from a distance.

We've always been opposites, Daniel and me, as different
as day and night. Back then I was pious, disciplined, obedient, and God-fearing. He was troubled, had a street mindset, and was already involved in the world of drugs and
crime. But I loved him, and he loved me. He was well-built,
very masculine and good-looking—he still he looks great for
his age—and at that time he had long braids he was real
proud of. He was very protective of his new younger brother, and he would often ask me if anyone was bothering me at
school or around where we lived. And I would always say,
"No," because I feared for the consequences if I named anybody. Still, it was nice to know that I had this protector in
my family.

But Daniel took drugs all the time he was living with us,

as he had at his foster-home, and his drug abuse got him into all sorts of ugly situations. Pretty soon he was robbing people at gun and knife-point. Later on he was taking stuff from the family home to sell to fund his habit. He got thrown out of a car going at a hundred miles an hour over some deal that went bad. He survived that, but things hit rock-bottom when my mother received a phone call at two o'clock one morning saying that Daniel had been shot in the head. He was alive, but he had been shot in the head. My mom woke me and my sister, packed us into the car, and we drove down to what was then called Memphis City Hospital sleepy-eyed and full of fear.

What I saw in that hospital was just incredible, and haunts me to this day—there were people with stab-wounds, people with gunshot wounds in them just sitting there, or leaning on walls, or laying on stretchers, or even on the floor, still and silent, or moaning in pain. There was blood in smears and pools on the floors, vivid red, and crusting and drying black. I watched people die waiting to be seen by a doctor because back then you had no right to medical attention unless you had plenty of insurance: if you didn't have insurance you just had to wait. And there was my brother, shot in the head, waiting with the rest of them. Dying. Eventually he was seen by a doctor, and they rushed him into surgery and operated on him, and mercifully he survived, though he has a steel plate permanently riveted into his skull as a consequence. To this day I don't know the exact circumstances around the shooting and, truth to tell, I don't want to know.

Despite her mental problems, my mom is fundamentally a very strong woman, and she held up good to start off with. She'd visit Daniel in the hospital every day after work to make sure he had what he needed, and when he came home she looked after him as best she could. But there's no question that all the things he had been doing leading up to the shooting had been wearing her down, and seeing him nearly die had almost been too much for her.

It was my sister who pushed her over the edge.

Nowadays my sister's a together person, and we're very close. She's made her journey in life and found her own way through some difficult times. She's hard-working and she's raised three daughters, all of whom have attended college. She's a success. But back then she was just selfish, and determined to get her own way, regardless of how much it hurt other people. Having been brought up in a loose, disorderly household, she resented my mother for attempting to discipline her.

At that time my sister was seeing a guy named 'Tyrone,' and she wanted to move in with him, even to marry him, but my mother insisted she was too young, and forbade it. My sister got so mad that she went to my cousin, who also lived in Memphis, and between the two of them they cooked up a scheme to take my mother to court, accuse her of not being a fit mother, and have my sister placed in my cousin's home. Then she could carry on her relationship with Tyrone as she pleased. What made this a particularly low thing to do was that they planned to make a series of false accusations of abuse and neglect against my mom and use her mental health history to discredit her. Both my brother and I knew my sister's accusations were false, but what could we do? I couldn't have been more than twelve, and although he was older, Daniel had his own problems with drugs to deal with and a criminal record, and by then wasn't living at home with us anyway.

So my sister took my mother to court, told a self-serving version of events, and was taken from our home and placed with my cousin. My mom felt hugely betrayed by both my sister and my cousin, and that, after what she had gone through with my brother, combined with the pressure from working two jobs and raising me on her own, was just too much for her. Slowly she began to break down. There was just me and her in the house. And although I never blamed her for it because I knew it was caused by her mental condition, at that time she did become physically and psychologically abusive towards me. It was usually over small-seeming things. For example, we had a large yard, and I would cut the grass with the lawnmower. If the lawnmower engine cut out for any reason while I was using it, she would come rushing out of the house and accuse me of deliberately breaking it to avoid cutting the lawn, and she would whip me. So there was that mixture of paranoia and rage inside her head a lot of the time, and it came rushing out more and more frequently. Yet because I loved her I didn't want to leave her. I didn't want to abandon our home. I didn't want to desert her as, one way or the other, my brother and sister had done. I tried to stay there and help her as best I could, but it became increasingly difficult as her mental state worsened.

I was regularly in touch with my foster-mother during all this time, which meant that I had some emotional and psy- chological support outside of my immediate biological fam- ily. Also there was an older lady who lived just up the road from us, who would look after me and my sister after school and during the holidays while my mom was out working. This lady was very loving and supportive, almost becoming a stand-in parent to me, and her kindness and generosity helped me cope with my difficult home situation. Also she had a beautiful grand-daughter called 'Judy,' whom I fell in love with. I would have been twelve, maybe just thirteen, at the time. To tell the truth it was kind of a Cinderella romance, as by then I was already developing strong feelings towards men, and in fact all the serious emotional relation- ships of my adult life would turn out to be with men, but Judy made life a little more sweet for me in a time that was turning increasingly bitter.

Around this time I also had my first sexual experience with another male. He was a friend of mine from the neigh- borhood, the same age as me. We were playing tree-house and all of a sudden he started rubbing up on me. It was a bold thing for him to do, and I guess I was surprised, but I liked it so I let him carry on. And he went down on me and the feeling was—whoah!—so good! It was a revelation. No one had ever done that to me before. And he had a girlfriend, and I had Judy, and Judy and his girlfriend were good friends. So that was something else that was going on at that time.

Another time a little after that I had an older guy

(handwritten margin note: "Vital in chaotic family sit")

approach me in a wooded area not far from my mom's house. We were down in the woods and he came on to me in this brazen way, saying, "I know you like it, I know you like it!" And I wasn't saying anything back to him because he was right: I *did* like it. He went down on me there among the bushes, and once again it was a hot experience. He was a black guy, and very attractive, and even though I was only twelve or so he said I already had a big dick.

A year later I had another experience that wasn't so enjoyable. I had been down to watch friends playing baseball in the local park and was walking home. It was around six in the evening, just getting dark, and I was passing by that same wooded area. I guess my thoughts were elsewhere, because I really didn't notice that someone was coming up behind me. A man. Instead of passing by me he put a knife to my back and whispered in my ear, "Go up in those bushes. You gon' suck my dick." His voice was thick and he sounded real nervous. A quick glance told me there was no one else around to see my situation: I was on my own with this guy. I could feel the sharp tip of the blade against my kidney so I knew he wasn't fooling and I let him hustle me into the darkness under the trees. I also knew I wasn't up for performing oral sex on him: if I was going to do something sexually, then I was going to do it freely or not at all.

I had already said in my mind, "I ain't gon' suck your dick, you gon' have to cut me first," so when he pulled his pants down I upped and hit him hard as I could. He was taller than me, and older and heavier, but he went down. I jumped to my feet and took off as fast as I could. But in the darkness I could hardly see where I was going, and I ran straight into a tree. I banged my face on the harsh bark of the trunk and cut open my forehead, splitting the skin over my eye and almost knocking myself out, but I managed to stagger back onto the street and hurry away before my pursuer could catch up to me.

When I got home my mom saw the cut over my eye and asked what had happened. I pretended I had made a mistake playing baseball and had been hit in the eye by one of the balls because I didn't want to tell her the truth. It's strange the shame you can feel at being the victim of a sexual assault, even one that's only attempted. *What was the problem? All vague*

Then had to be some diagnosis from at this time. Was it genetic As my mother's mental health declined she became *which did out for the brothers doing well* resentful of the amount of time I was spending at Judy's grandmother's house, and tried to stop me from seeing her or Judy, and my fledgling romance was ended as what little was left of my family life collapsed around my ears. My mom also tried to prevent me speaking to my foster-mother. I guess my being close to either my foster-mother or Judy's grandmother made her feel like even more of a failure as a parent than she was feeling already.

At this point the cracks were becoming too numerous for me to paper over, and I eventually confided my situation to the counselor at my school, Westwood Junior High. He put me in touch with someone at family services. That person encouraged me to try and stick out the academic year but in the end I just couldn't cope with both continuing my studies and dealing with the situation at home any longer. One time my mom just vanished from the house completely, and it was then that through family services I went to court to ask the judge to return me to my foster-mother.

Later on I found out that, once I had left the family home and my mother had been institutionalized again, my cousins had turned up at the house, let themselves in and moved all of my mother's furniture and possessions over to my cousin's house. That was how come my brother Daniel finally fell out with my sister: he felt that she had treated my mother so badly he wanted nothing more to do with her.

When we got close again, many years later, my sister opened up to me and confided that what she had done back then had been the worst mistake of her life: Tyrone dropped her and married someone else, and it turned out that not only had my cousin's (now ex-) husband been molesting one of his own daughters, he also began sleeping with May shortly after she moved in. So my sister reaped what she sowed, unfortunately for her.

My mom never fully recovered from her breakdown, although these days she's doing better than she was. She now lives in an assisted living unit in St. Louis, near to my sister, and May and I both help support her financially, and visit her, so I guess in the end May has made up for some of the hurt she caused.

When I went to court I was assuming that the State would return me to my foster-mother, who clearly stated that she wanted to have me back home with her again. To this day I don't know why my request to be placed with her was denied. But it was. Instead I was sent to a state institution for

orphaned, troubled, and homeless children 210 miles away:
Tennessee Preparatory School.

CHAPTER THREE:

FATHER

Where was my father in all this? Nowhere. In all the time I was growing up I met him only once, when he came by the house at my mother's instigation. Not because she wanted to see him—she certainly didn't—but because she felt it was important for a son to know his father. She warned me to expect nothing of him, to not believe any promises he might make to visit again or take me out for treats or on trips, and she was right.

The best I can say about my father is that he was never the settling-down kind. He owned his own construction business, was married seven times and had, to my knowledge, between twenty-five and thirty children. I owe him for bringing me into the world, but that's about it. He never supported my mother or us children either emotionally or financially, and who knows how different our lives might have been had he done so. But I have never used my father's utter indifference towards me or my mother as an excuse or a crutch to explain away failings in my own life. My adoptive father, my foster-mother's grandson, is the man who truly raised me, and he taught me to step up to the plate and take responsibility for my own life, and this I have always striven to do.

I would have been twelve years old the day my father came by the house. He was a very masculine-looking man, hard-bodied, and very muscular. Even today he looks good for his age, and both me and my brother get a lot of our genes from him, which is our good fortune. But once again here I was being confronted by a total stranger. There was no moment of deep recognition. All I knew about this man was that he had never wanted me. He had never done one thing for me, my brother, my sister, or my mother, other than get our mother pregnant. And right away he started in with lies about why he had never been involved in our lives. I listened, and I was polite, and he left, and that was that.

We could have a relationship now, perhaps, as one man to another, but not a daddy-son relationship. He can never be "Dad" to me: it's too late for that. But if he needed something, really needed something, I would help him if I could. For he is my father, after all, although he was no father to me.

Ironically he did do one thing for me that turned out to be important for my own mental well-being later on, because it was through him that I learned of a half-brother I had over in Dallas. I got in touch with this half-brother, and we subsequently became very close, and he was able to help me deal with a lot of the anger I felt towards our father. He encouraged me to let go of it and accept him for what he is: a flawed human being with good as well as bad in him. Eventually I managed to do so. But at the time I could do nothing with my anger except pray that it wouldn't make my heart bitter.

CHAPTER FOUR:

TENNESSEE PREPARATORY SCHOOL

In 1873, Memphis was stricken by a cholera epidemic in which hundreds of people died, and as a consequence many children were left orphans. A philanthropic judge named John C. Ferriss petitioned the Tennessee State Legislature to establish a boarding school for the care and education of those orphans. When his petition was rejected by the Legislature he turned to private subscriptions to raise the money to start such a school.

One man who gave money to fund the school was Colonel Edmund W. Cole, who initially donated $1,000, which was a considerable sum of money back then, but still not enough to buy the land and build and equip the buildings and so, despite his generosity, and despite other people also giving smaller sums, the project initially floundered.

However, Colonel Cole had a son named Randall. In October, 1884, Randall, who was only nineteen years old, was severely injured in a train-derailment. He died from his injuries shortly after he was pulled from the wreckage, and a grief-stricken Colonel Cole decided that he would turn the Cole family mansion into a memorial to his deceased son, and used what would have been Randall's inheritance to establish on February 20th, 1885, the Randall Cole Industrial School "for the benefit & protection of orphan, helpless, or abandoned children."

By 1887 the school was too large for Colonel Cole to manage so he turned it over to the State of Tennessee free of charge, at which time it became known as the Tennessee Industrial School. The State assessed the annual cost of keeping a child at the school at that time as $150; $50 came from the county, $50 from the state, and the child would earn the remaining $50 from working on the school farm.

In 1921 Christian Menzler became head of the school. He reorganized & improved it, making it one of the most outstanding of its kind in the U.S. In 1955 it became the Tennessee Preparatory School. It was to this school that I was sent at the age of fourteen. I was to remain there for nearly two years.

To quote from the description of the school on its alumnus website, Tennessee Preparatory School was "probably the most misunderstood school in Tennessee. It was *not* a reformatory or treatment center. It was a place that provided a home and education for the children of Tennessee who did not have the privilege of having those things in a family setting. It allowed abused, neglected, and underprivileged children to be children again. The school had one of the best academic curricula in Tennessee, a superb athletic program, an excellent vocational program, and many clubs where the kids could be kids."

TPS was in Nashville, the state capitol of Tennessee, and was a three hour drive from Memphis. I had never been as far from home as Nashville before, so it was unknown territory to me. Along with several other young boys I was taken from the juvenile court and put in a white mini-van for transportation. It was clean and comfortable, and there were no bars on the windows or anything that made it seem at all prison-van-like, but still I was unhappy: I had gone to court to get myself returned to the care of my foster-mother, and now here I was being sent away from everyone and everything I knew to an unfamiliar institution that sounded almost like a jail, in a strange city, by order of the State.

In fact, despite my fears, TPS was more like a regular high school or college than any sort of reformatory. Its mostly old buildings were scattered across a huge campus that sprawled out over ninety-three acres of grounds. It was like a small city, a little world all on its own. We had a recreation hall, we had a cafeteria which served surprisingly good food; we even had our own movie theatre. There was a church on campus, and I attended services there every Sunday. We lived in single-sex dormitories, with the girls' dorms on one side of the campus, the boys' on the other, and there was a campus security force whose main task was to keep the boys and girls from getting together. We even had a tiny jail for miscreants. There were younger children living there too: they didn't stay in the dorms with the older ones, but were housed on another part of the campus. It was very racially mixed.

On arriving I was assigned to a dormitory, along with the other new boys. The dorms were assigned by sex and district, and since I was from Memphis and I was a boy I was assigned to a dorm called Browning Hall. Having always had a bedroom of my own as a child, you can imagine it was quite scary to suddenly find myself in a huge dormitory, sharing my living and sleeping space with upwards of sixty other boys, all of whom were strangers to me.

Despite having witnessed my mother's nervous break-down and my brother's gunshot wound to the head, I was in the main a sheltered child. I had been brought up for most of my life in a loving, orderly, and pious family situation. My foster-mother cared for me and supervised me closely. I did my chores. I read my Bible. I studied hard in school. I had never had a serious fight. I had never smoked or drunk alcohol or used drugs. And here I was, all of a sudden, amongst kids who had been neglected and abused, kids who had mental problems, kids who had been involved in low-level criminal activities such as shop-lifting and the like. To say the least, it was an eye-opening time for me.

At first I kept to myself and just observed. There were moments when it all became too much for me and I had to shed some tears. Being raised up in the church I prayed a lot, and that gave me some strength. Also I would speak to my foster-mother regularly on the telephone and, as I knew she was going through the courts to try and get me back to live with her, that lifted me up a little. The legal process involved in getting me out of TPS turned out to be extremely lengthy and difficult, but knowing that my foster-mother wanted me back living with her helped me through some difficult times emotionally. Sometimes she would send me money so I could visit her on weekends, a four hundred and twenty mile round journey, so I didn't lose touch with her or with my friends and associates in Memphis altogether.

As time passed I got more confident and opened up. I made friends, and started to have some fun. I studied hard, I worked—everyone there worked to earn their keep as well as attending school—and I played football and basketball and ran track and cross-country. I loved football but it was in running track and cross-country that I really excelled, building somewhat of a name for myself, breaking some local records and becoming a track star.

In many ways TPS echoed the values my foster-mother had brought me up with: industry, self-discipline, and paying your own way. We students would do summer jobs. We would work in the administrative offices. We would strip the floors at the school to keep them clean. TPS also had on-campus counselors who you could talk problems through with any time you needed to. My favorite counselor was a Miss Wilson, a very nice lady, who I think liked me because I was reared up to respect rules and regulations, and supported and advised me as best she could. And I had many helpful talks with Doctor Jack Lumbar, the superintendent, up in his office.

From which you can deduce I was never a slick child. But still I managed to have me some fun. For instance, there was a girl at the school named 'Mabel,' a fine-looking girl, and

I'd heard a lot about her and her easy-going ways. One day, during football practice, I was out on the field and I had to go back to the dressing-room for something I'd forgotten. I entered the dressing-room and went through to the bathroom, and there was my friend from Browning Hall, 'Alex', and he and Mabel were fucking in there. They saw me come in and they knew I could see them plain as day, but they just carried right on with what they were doing as if they couldn't care less. Now, I could have done a number of things at that point, I guess, but I thought to myself, "Why not get me some of this?" and I went over and joined them and we ended up in a threesome, me and Alex both fucking Mabel at the same time. It was moments like that that made TPS a fun place to be!

At one point I was dating a really gorgeous girl named 'Letitia', and another friend of mine from Browning Hall, 'Ronald', was dating a girl named 'Nicky'. As I've already mentioned, the authorities would do all they could to keep male and female students apart, but young love—or lust—finds a way, and there was a lot of sex between the girls and the boys. There were pregnancies too, though to my knowledge I never got a girl pregnant. Both Nicky and Letitia were from Memphis, and I still see them occasionally, all these years later, and we talk about the past, and our time at TPS. They're both married now. Last time I saw Nicky she said, "You doing might good, your sexy acts in all those movies!" I was surprised she knew about my films and I told her so. She laughed and said, "I knew all about you, even back then. I always knew you was bisexual." And of course she was right, and of course at the same time I was dating Letitia I was also having an affair with a guy who was in Browning Hall with me. His name was 'Andre'.

Now the halls were like gangs, or stand-in families: us guys from Browning Hall would look out for each other and protect each other. And Andre first represented himself to me as a protector: our relationship started off with him hanging out with me, saying stuff like, "I'm your big brother, ain't nobody gon' bother you when I'm around," and it went on from there to become an affair. He was maybe two years older than me. He was a very masculine brother, and was well-liked by everyone on the campus. He had the body of a Greek god and was a running-back on the football team. He was gorgeous—always well-groomed, and his jeans were always neatly-ironed and his clothes well-kept—and like me he had been raised up in a foster-home. We became very, very close the time I was there, though we lost touch when I left TPS, and I often wonder how he's doing today.

As you would expect there were rivalries between the different halls, and that's what led to the first serious fight of my life, which took place in the school cafeteria. Each dorm had to take turns working in the kitchen, running it for a month, keeping it clean, washing the dishes and serving food to the other students and staff, and that time it was Browning Hall's turn. This would have been not long after I had arrived at TPS. I was behind the counter serving up eggs or something and I guess I didn't put enough food on this one boy's plate, because he got mad and threw the plate at me, food and all. I moved aside sharply and it flew on by and smashed against the wall behind me, sending shards of pottery and mess flying everywhere. This kid was from Hudson Hall and I knew at once I couldn't let his disrespectful action towards me pass as we had a rivalry going on. The other kids from Hudson Hall were watching me to see what I would do, and so were my boys from Browning Hall. Right then and there, sheltered as I was, I knew I had to beat this other kid down: I knew that if I didn't beat him half to death I would never have any respect from my boys. So I did it. I surprised myself. It wasn't something I knew I could even do: beat someone that badly. But I did it, and after that I was never bothered again.

The college security force broke up the fight, and I ended up in the little jail they had on campus. But only for one night.

Gradually TPS became home to me. We worked together, we went to school together, and we played sports together. We laughed and we looked out for each other. We disagreed with each other, but we really did become one big happy family. It was my home for nearly two years, and over that time it really did become home in the most genuine sense of the word.

Three years ago I went back to Tennessee Prep. I wanted to revisit the place that had been such a part of my life and had meant so much to me. But by then they no longer housed kids there, and most of the buildings where we had studied and played sports, watched movies and worked, were leased out as cheap office-space to various government departments. Most of the dorms had been torn down. It was a ghost of a place, its educational and caring roles deemed obsolete by the State of Tennessee, and I felt deeply saddened at the sight of the institution that had done so much for me being slowly taken down and pulled apart.

CHAPTER FIVE:

A HOMECOMING, A PASSING, AND A NEW START

All the time I was at Tennessee Preparatory School my fos-ter-mother was going through the courts to get me back to live with her. I don't know why it should have been such a lengthy, drawn-out process, given that my real mother didn't challenge my foster-mother's claim on me. Perhaps my real mom's mental fragility made it difficult to sort things out quickly. Perhaps it was just the slow grinding of the mills of state bureaucracy. Whatever the reason, it wasn't until the age of fifteen that I was finally removed from TPS and returned to my foster-mother's home in Orange Mound, back in Memphis.

I should say here that, despite all the dramas and difficul-ties with my real mother, my foster-mother always believed I should have a close relationship with her and my biological brother and sister, and supported my involvement with them. She met and got to know my real mother and sister and they became quite close. I count myself blessed in that way because I know that many fostered and adopted children have to deal with a lot of conflict and pain around the issue of blood ties, and whether their "real" parents are those that raised them or those to whom they are biologically related. I never had that conflict, because even in difficult times I always had some sort of supportive and loving family network around me, biological or non-biological.

It was a happy homecoming for me. Despite having to say goodbye so abruptly to all the friends I had made at TPS, I was overjoyed to be reunited with my foster-mother, and to be back in the house I had grown up in.

Our household had shrunk to just the two of us, as my foster-mother was long widowed, and my foster-brother Bobby was grown and had gone out into the world, but we were happy. Our reunion was to be short-lived, however. My foster-mother had been having heart problems for some time. They worsened rapidly, and less than a year after I had been returned to her care, she passed away. She was eighty-seven years old, but still her passing was deeply painful for me.

And there I was, at that moment, alone.

I would have been seriously worried about what was going to happen to me next—I was only fifteen, after all—if, on her death-bed, my foster-mother hadn't asked her grandson—my foster-nephew, who you will recall was considerably older than me—to "make sure my boy's taken care of." Her grandson more than honored her last request, because he and his wife not only took care of me, they went so far as to legally adopt me. So I went from being my foster-nephew's uncle to being his adopted son. To this day I'm so grateful that he would do that for me.

After the funeral I moved in with my adoptive father and mother and their young daughter, who of course instantly became my baby sister. Both my father and mother are successful business people, and at that time they lived in an area of mid-town Memphis called Central Gardens. Central Gardens is a well-off residential district with spacious, Victorian-style homes and its own private security force. It's also pretty much all white; at that time we were one of only two African-American families living there, so I knew from the moment I first arrived that I was moving into a neighborhood that the average African-American in the city of Memphis would never experience.

When my friends from Orange Mound would come by our house they would always say, "Oh, y'all rich!" Now, I could understand why they said that—we ran expensive cars, we were living in a large, well-maintained four-level house, we had a housekeeper who cleaned and cooked for us and a yard-man who kept the garden looking good—but I would always insist that we really *weren't* rich: my parents were just hard-working professional people who were careful with their money.

We had a fluffy little dog called Brandy, a real beautiful little girl, a Cocker Spaniel, who I used to walk round the neighborhood. Sometimes I'd be stopped by the private security guards, who would ask what I was doing "round here." They wouldn't want to believe it when I pointed to our house and told them, "I'm walking my dog and I live right over there."

It was bare-faced racism, of course. I told my mom and dad about it and they listened and said, "Well, you just have to expect a little bit of that in an area like this." They were realists. They didn't make a big deal of it, so I was able to laugh it off rather than becoming scarred by it or bitter over it. And I should add that, although we did have an older white neighbor across the street who was somewhat preju-diced, mostly people were friendly towards us and we didn't have many problems.

When Brandy died—she was pretty old and had gotten arthritis by the time she passed—we had a proper funeral service for her out at the dog cemetery, with a little casket, and flowers, and prayers and hymns just like you'd have for a human. I thought it was so cute. When I told some of my friends from back in Orange Mound about it, they laughed and rolled their eyes and said, "Lord, them rich people even had a funeral for the *dog!*"

From the first I loved my little sister. She was my heart, and today we're still close. She's a very educated woman now, with two master's degrees. As kids we always got along real well. We were basically good kids, but despite our parents both believing in the same disciplinarian approach to child-rearing my foster-mother had used, in certain respects we were quite spoiled, and we could be real mischievous. Like for instance we told lies on our housekeeper and got her fired.

One of the rules of the house was that, once the house-keeper had done the washing-up, then if you dirtied a plate you washed it yourself. Well, we would dirty up plates, not wash them, leave them in the sink and then say the house-keeper wasn't doing her job. We would mess up the bath-rooms and say she hadn't cleaned them, and in the end she was fired over it. That backfired on us because my parents didn't hire a new housekeeper: they just told me and my sister that from now on we would have to do all the chores round the house. You would have thought we'd have learned from that but we didn't: we told lies on the yard-man too and he got let go as well. And once the yard-man was gone we had to tend to the yard on top of tidying the house.

For my schooling I was sent to Green Haven High, an almost entirely all-white school over in East Memphis. Westwood Junior High, the school my real mom had sent me to when I was living with her, was pretty much all black, and while I was there I had been a straight "A" student. At Green Haven High I had to work much harder to excel, which came as somewhat of a shock to me, but I was bright and hard-working, and I enjoyed the challenge.

It was the first time I had been in an environment where white people were the vast majority. It was also the first time

I met people whose parents were doctors or lawyers or other professionals, or ran substantial businesses such as catering concerns or chains of pizza restaurants. Along with my experiences at TPS this meant that I learned to get along with a wide range of people from a fairly early age. This ability to approach people on their own level was to be very useful to me when I entered the world of adult entertainment: I never felt intimidated or out of my depth.

My parents were ambitious for me and my sister's education, and at one point they wanted to send me to an upscale private school for boys called Christian Brothers. My sister's experience of being at a similar private school for girls, Saint Mary's, had been an unhappy one, however, and since I didn't want to go to a single-sex school anyway, I said I would rather continue on at Green Haven High. Wanting first and foremost for me to be happy, my parents allowed me to do so.

A. Inability of children to see consequences. Solely dictated by their impulses, altho at his age 15† shd have known that lying in this way was reprehensible

CHAPTER SIX:

LIFE
LESSONS

I enjoyed English, math, and history. Math I found very difficult but the teacher was incredibly patient with me and so I achieved good grades.

The lessons I learned at Green Haven High were not all academic, however. In my history class the teacher, who was a man, came on to me. By then I had some friends a few years older than me who were gay and they told me that this teacher was not only gay but had a boyfriend he lived with. I was a bit naïve back then, so I was surprised when he made a move on me. "But he already has a lover," I thought to myself, all innocence and romance, not yet having learned what dogs men can be.

Boyfriend or not, I didn't find him at all attractive sexually, so I turned him down flat.

That evening I told my dad about the incident. He kept a level head and said I should always remember I never had to do anything I didn't want to, and to tell him if it ever happened again. I guess by then I was sixteen and no longer a child, if not yet a man, and my father knew I wasn't a natural victim.

That teacher had a little room at back of his classroom, and one time I went back there after class for some reason or other and saw him on his knees going down on another boy. They didn't see me though, so I just snuck away quietly.

At around the same time that happened I was having sex with another of my teachers, a very attractive woman of about thirty who taught the sociology class. It was purely a sexual thing for both of us: she didn't want a relationship with me, and I didn't want one with her. She would give me money, and she even bought me clothes—jeans, shirts, stuff like that. I never went to her home, though: like my history teacher she had a room at back of her classroom, and we would fuck in there. I never told anyone about it while it was happening. A gentleman doesn't kiss and tell, and I was never one of those teenagers who felt a need to brag about his conquests to his fellows.

[handwritten margin note: What were these teachers drinking? Rather annoying typography with it]

Since I was doing exactly what I wanted, the phrase "statutory rape" never entered my mind, any more than it did when I saw my history teacher going down on one of my male classmates.

We carried on like that for about a year, me and my sociology teacher. Then I moved on to the next grade and it was over.

I used to have sex with a lot of the girls I went to Green Haven with, too, mostly in the school bathroom. Back then

I had long hair down my back, and for some reason girls seem to like guys with long hair. I never knew any of them to fall pregnant as a result of our fun times together, but even now I wouldn't be surprised to find out that I had fathered a child by one of them that I never knew about.

From an early age I would find myself getting attention from both women and men on account of my athletic build. I was always naturally muscular—owing to my father's genes—and I was fit, and because I had been playing football from the time I was in junior high my legs were real big. I had Herschel Walker legs, and I liked to show them off. As well as playing football I was running track, the half-a-mile and the mile, and cross-country, and after school I would train by running in the streets of Memphis in real tight shorts. It was crazy because guys would drive by me, slow down and look me over in the most obvious way. Sometimes they'd blow me kisses from their open car windows and then speed away. Or they'd sound their horns to get my attention, pull over and engage me in conversation, and in the course of chit-chatting they'd ask me for directions to a certain street I had a feeling they already knew the way to. And I would always tell them I didn't know, because although I was still kind of naïve at that point as to what exactly that street signified, I was on the way to having a pretty good idea.

Still, I loved the attention. *the attributes of all teenagers when inflated egos are fragile*

I was at the table with my mom and dad eating supper one evening when my mom asked me point-blank if I was gay. I told her no. I would have only been sixteen, and at that time I was somewhat in denial about my sexuality. I wasn't yet comfortable in it, and certainly I didn't feel comfortable talking to my parents about it. What teenager, gay, straight, or bisexual, wants to discuss his sex life with his parents?

There was a long, pregnant pause, then my father said, "Well, we know you're gay. We have gay friends, and the only thing we require you to do is be honest with yourself, and respectful to yourself."

I was extremely touched and moved by my father's words. I know so many gay people, especially young gay people, whose parents have rejected them on account of their sexuality, even thrown them out into the street like garbage. I opened up to my dad and my mom then, and they have both been incredibly supportive of me in everything I've done since, from my involvement in the adult movie business to relationships. There are times when I've been down, had my heart broken, and I've put my head on my father's shoulder and cried. He and my mother have been a stronghold for me, and I thank God for them, because I know everybody don't have that.

Being as I was so masculine, and had been dating so many girls, you might wonder what made my parents think I was gay in the first place. It's true I was also dating a guy on the football team, but they didn't know about that: nobody did.

Partly it was small, almost subliminal things, I guess. Glances in the rear-view mirror. Like I remember driving with my mom and dad through Memphis and passing places I could tell were gay from the patrons hanging outside them. I took note of those places mentally, and I guess my parents noticed me taking note and it made them think.

Not only that, but my mom became aware that I seemed to be getting sick of girls. Because I was on the football team—I was wide receiver, second team quarterback—and was also breaking local records for track and cross-country, I was very popular at school: my name was always coming over the loudspeaker with the announcement I had broken this record or that record, and like any sports star I had groupies. Girl groupies. They would buy me Levi's just to hear me putting 'em on in the changing room cubicles in the stores and see me wearing them. Well, that was okay; I was happy enough for my groupies to buy me jeans, but they were forever pestering me for dates as well. It got to the point where these girls were calling me up at home all the time, and it wore me down. I wouldn't answer the phone. I'd let my mom answer, and when she asked me what she should say to them I'd say, "Tell them I'm in Africa doing missionary work." So I guess that got my mom thinking, "Well, he doesn't like girls."

Also there were these twins named 'Danny' and 'Donnie', two fellow-students who started coming over to visit me, who were towards the effeminate end of the scale. I was actually seeing Donnie for a while, but it didn't last long because even then I didn't really like "soft" guys. So my mom picked up on them as well as other guys I was meeting at that time who would come by the house. And all these things led to her asking me about my sexuality round the dinner table that particular evening.

A year or so after that I stepped more fully into what you would call the gay world. I would have been seventeen. My parents were out of town for the weekend, and I left the house and went by this gay bar that was within walking distance of where we lived. It was called The Other Side, and was on Cleveland and Madison.

Was I going to go in?

I didn't know. I didn't have a plan.

As it turned out I didn't have to make that decision, because standing outside of the bar I saw this gorgeous man. He was black, a bodybuilder, and he had this amazing physique and an ass that went on for *days*.

I was shy but I was bold—I went straight up to him. We struck up a conversation. One thing led to another, and I took him home and I took him to my bedroom and I made love to him. I fucked him for three hours *straight*.

It was a turning point for me because, although it wasn't the first time I had penetrated another man, it was the first time I had penetrated a man that big, and it was one of the most amazing experiences I had ever had in my life. Big, muscular, masculine men who love being fucked became my ideal from then on in.

Like my friends from Orange Mound he took one look at my house and said, "Damn, you're rich!"

Afterwards we got dressed and I walked him back to the bar. Then I came back home, my dick and thighs aching, feeling light and wild and free.

After that I became very curious about the gay scene. I started going to gay bars and clubs on a regular basis.

Back then there were a lot of clubs in Memphis, both gay and straight. Despite its reputation for conservatism and

Puritanism, in those days Memphis was booming as a fun city. It was the happening place to be, and people would come there from as far away as New York to have a good time. The best-known gay clubs at that time were the Apartment Club, The Other Side, The Bath-House and Jay-Wag. The Apartment Club had a mostly African-American clientele; The Other Side was more of a mixed crowd.

It wasn't just about having a good time, though: it was also about community, gay community. Because back then homosexuality wasn't so much accepted by the African-American community, and many black gay men and black lesbians were rejected by their families. So they came together at gay bars and clubs, men and women both, and strong bonds were forged between them. This man would become my brother, this woman would become my sister. We would become a family for those whose families had turned them away. So the other club I want to mention here is one that ran on Sundays which was called The Family Affair. They would put on shows there, and the legendary female impersonator Miss Peaches would perform.

Although I don't hold with the notion that if you're a gay man you need to twist and turn and adopt feminine mannerisms, I have great respect for Miss Peaches. She was a forebear for the gay community here in Memphis. When the city had parades she would appear in them and teach the kids how to be majorettes and stuff like that. She opened doors for others to be accepted. I remember meeting her and thought her a very nice person. She was very popular, and although she died many years ago, she's still well-remembered here.

The Family Affair was located on Vance Avenue, which was in a real bad neighborhood. It was mostly a lesbian club. There weren't many lesbian clubs, and as the women didn't have much variety to choose from, they would sometimes come to where the guys were at. They weren't always welcome, though. Not because they were women but because for some reason, especially down here in the South, the women fight a lot. They would fight like *soldiers*. And the guys, they didn't like being around all of that brawling and beating. But down at The Family Affair the men and women mixed in and mostly got along fine.

At the bars and clubs I met a lot of very handsome guys: numerous guys would come on to me and, unlike with the girl groupies from school, I loved it. I was the center of attention, and it suited me fine.

People often ask me if I started acting in gay porn movies to get attention, but that was never the reason: I was already getting plenty of the attention I wanted without being in front of a camera. Acting in porn was about something else altogether.

Although I'm known for being a gay porn-star, I define myself as bisexual. When I tell people that, they sometimes ask me if, since I'm bisexual, I could be in a relationship with a woman. In fact I have dated women. But in my experience they're too controlling: they want to know your every whereabout, and it's just too much for me. It's not that I want to go out and have fun, fun, fun all the time, particularly as I get older, but I enjoy my quiet time. I enjoy space. I enjoy my freedom, my ability to come and go as I please. And although I've had male partners who have been both jealous and controlling, I feel a man is more likely to understand my need for a particular type of personal freedom. So it's probably no accident that all the serious romantic relationships of my adult life have been with men.

My involvement in the gay scene was a big distraction from my studies at school, and my academic career began to suffer as a result. I had no plans for what I was going to do once I finished school, and was really only interested in having a good time.

As graduation neared my father sat me down to discuss what I wanted to do with my life. I was vague.

He said, "If you're going to stay here then you're going to go to college. And if you don't go to college then you're going to have to get out of my house."

"Wow," I thought. "That's harsh." I thought he was being mean. But he went on, "I still love you, but you're going to have to be a man now and stand on your own feet." If I went to college he would support me. If I didn't then I would have to get a job and move out and take full responsibility for my own life.

That was something I didn't feel quite ready to do at that point. So that fall I began attending a local community college, not because I was strongly motivated to study, but for want of anything better to do. I did have vague thoughts of becoming a policeman, but I was never focused enough to pursue law-enforcement as a career. I guess the nearest I came to it was in the gay adult movie *Soul Patrol*, where I played a cop dealing with burglars and the like.

Don't get me wrong, though; while I wasn't the most dedicated student in the world I was never idle. I studied fairly hard and I helped pay my way through my first year of college by working as a sacker in a local grocery store called Cecil's. I would take basic classes in the mornings and then work in Cecil's in the afternoons. And in the evenings I would go out to bars and clubs and stay out late having a good time.

I lasted a year at college. If I hadn't been so wrapped up in the gay scene I reckon I'd have two Ph.D. degrees by now, but it just didn't happen that way. Now, more than quarter of a century later, I've come full circle, and am studying for a law degree, but back then I was more interested in going out and having fun.

I moved out of my parents' house, and they helped me set up home in a small one-bed apartment in the mid-town area of Memphis. It was on Jefferson Street, which in those days was the place to be. Twenty-seven years later it's really gone downhill, but back then it was an upscale area, and I loved living there.

That first time living on my own I didn't manage money very well: I got credit cards and maxed them out, fell behind with the rent, and was going to be evicted as a result. My parents had warned me about the importance of choosing my friends well, but unfortunately I didn't heed their warning, and when my money ran out and I needed help all my so-called friends vanished, leaving me stranded and broke. I really didn't want to go to my parents and beg them to bail me out, but in the end it was all I could do.

After threatening to let me be turned out into the street to teach me a lesson they did help me out, of course. But I learned my lesson, and since then I've always managed my money sensibly. My mother cut up my credit cards and I didn't replace them until I was financially back on my feet.

Seeing the mess I had gotten myself into, my parents let me move back in with them until I could get enough money saved up to strike out on my own again.

Fortunately, in the meantime I had found a way I could earn a decent living that fit with my club and bar-oriented lifestyle: dancing.

CHAPTER SEVEN:

MISTER
WONDERFUL

The first time I danced it was for a dare, but the moment I stepped up onto the platform I found that I loved it, being up there in front of a crowd showing off my body.

I've never felt it was appropriate to be working in the porn industry at the same time as being prominent or active in the church. I've always kept the two apart. But I don't feel the same way about dancing. Why not display your body if you've worked hard to sculpt it and make it beautiful to look at? It seems to me that the people who most object to displaying the body are those who are eaten up with envy— physically unattractive themselves, they try to damn what they lack with the charge of immorality.

I was a good dancer. I had a good physique, and I loved the attention that dancing in bars and clubs brought me. At first I was just doing it for fun and wasn't thinking of it as a way I could generate an income. But as I went on more and more people started coming to me and saying that I had what it took to earn a living that way. Certainly there were no other jobs that I had any desire to do, and it would have been around that time that I found myself back in my parents' house, flat broke and with no other prospects.

So I started working out seriously to build bulk and get cut, and dancing became what I did for a living. It was to take me all over the country, and it paid me good money, sometimes very good money. It was also a form of art to me, a way of expressing myself that I very much enjoyed. It amazes me even to this day how I was such a sickly little baby and yet I went on to develop a physique, a body that has taken me not only all around the country but also all over the world.

I started dancing at the Apartment Club in Memphis and went on from there. As well as being paid a fee for each show I did, appreciative patrons would put tips in my thong. On top of that I would get asked for private dances, for which I would get paid extra. Private dances weren't supposed to tip over into anything directly sexual but, human nature being what it is, they quite often did. Living as I was in such a sexualized world, I had no problem with that, providing I found the patron attractive.

So pretty rapidly I found myself making a fair bit of money as well as showing off my body and enjoying myself.

I had some wild times back then. I had sex in the clubs, of course. I've had sex on a plane. I've had sex on a train. I've had sex in a bus. I've fucked the most gorgeous guys you can imagine. I've had sex with a married man in his home, and had to hide in the attic when his wife walked in the house.

People assume Memphis to be one of the strictest, most conservative cities in the country, but as I've already said, it wasn't so. We had bath-houses, five or six different gay clubs, including one that would stay open twenty-four hours a day, seven days a week, while over in Atlanta, which is a notorious party town, clubs closed down.

We were having fun.

We didn't think whether what we were doing was right or wrong. We didn't take the time to think anything through: we were just living wild and free. We were ignorant of the facts and sometimes lacking in plain common sense. We would get into foolish and dangerous situations with alluring but crazy strangers. But mostly God kept us safe in the midst of it all. You know, even now I can't help but look back on those times as good times, despite knowing what we now know, that AIDS was just around the corner, and so many of those I knew then are gone today.

We weren't just hooking up at the clubs and bath-houses—in those days you could find yourself some fun just about anywhere.

One of the wildest places for sex in Memphis was Overton Park. Overton Park is in the center of Memphis and features a zoo, the Brooks Museum of Art, and a nine-hole golf course. Mostly though it's one hundred and seventy acres of forest—mainly great old oaks and hickories—and is riddled with trails for hiking and biking that in spring are lined with trillium, may-apples, and wild phlox.

The trails, the dense woodland, and the lack of

streetlights made for a great cruising ground, and back then it was known as a gay park. It was notorious. Central Park in New York had nothing on Overton! You went there and you could get whatever you needed—men of all types, all races were there, hanging out on the trails and in the bushes.

I preferred sex in the park to going back to some guy's house; going to a stranger's home can put you in harm's way, and you never know when they'll produce a wife or girlfriend to create a scene. So many men are liars and hypocrites.

The park was real nice in those days, but of course there were a lot of complaints about all the fucking that was going on up in there. That led to barriers being put up to stop you driving through, and then the city hired rangers. They would patrol the trails on horseback in search of things that were going on.

One time I was in the park fucking this professional wrestler I had met there. Most wrestlers have big, muscular asses and he was no exception, and there I was fucking his ass, happy as a pig in shit, when suddenly through the foliage I thought I saw a movement. At first I wondered if maybe it was my imagination but no, it was a ranger—a female ranger on horseback. We locked eyes and she yelled, "Halt!"

Well, the park rangers had radios but I knew they didn't have guns, so I pulled out, pulled up my pants, and ran. I vanished into the dense undergrowth and left her and that goddamned horse as far behind as I could. I was damned if *she* was going to take me to jail.

That wasn't the closest call I had in the park, though. That came when I was having this thing with the son of a big

Memphis attorney who is now a judge. It was two o'clock in the morning, black-dark. We had our pants round our ankles, I was fucking him, and we said to each other that if we saw a headlight coming our way we would just put on our clothes real fast.

So there I was fucking this attorney's son when all of a sudden the green lights come on and there was a damn police car right behind us! I hadn't seen or heard nothing; it was as if it had appeared out of nowhere. I guess I'd been too caught up in the moment.

I was so damned scared I couldn't pull my pants up; it was as if someone was holding my hands down by my side.

The two officers came up to us.

"What are you punks doing?" one of them demanded. Of course he knew exactly what we'd been doing.

"Nothing, sir," I said, sounding as humble as I could.

"Well, why in the fuck you punks got your clothes off?" he asked.

"I don't know, sir," I said.

All this time I was glancing over at the attorney's son thinking to myself, "Oh, shit, his father's gon' be mad, our ass is gon' be in the newspapers. My dad's gon' beat the shit out of me."

I couldn't see any way out of the situation so I just stood there, trying not to antagonize the police because at that moment they had power over me.

The other officer was checking our IDs to make sure that we didn't have any wants out on us, that we weren't criminals. Grudgingly he handed them back to us.

"Y'all get your punk motherfuckin' asses out of this park!"
And I said, "Yes, sir!" And I was *gone*.

Believe me, I was damn glad to leave that park that night!

That was my scariest moment, but mostly we had a lot of wild times and no regrets. I guess because I'd had this sheltered, shielded life for so many years I had a need to let my hair down and just have fun.

One aspect of the exciting new world I found myself in that didn't appeal to me, however, was the need for stimulants that afflicts so many gay men. Due to my strict Methodist upbringing I've never touched alcohol, I've never taken drugs, I've never even smoked cigarettes. To this day I couldn't be involved with a smoker—who wants to kiss someone with ashtray breath?—nor could I date someone who abused drugs or alcohol, though I have in the past had to cope with lovers who did both.

Any abuse of the body, whether it be drugs, drink, cigarettes or just slovenly neglect, lack of personal hygiene or obesity, totally turns me off. To me it represents self-hatred, and if you hate yourself how can you love someone else?

I was lucky when I started out dancing because it was something far fewer men wanted to do back then than they do today.

Like most exotic dancers I usually danced on my own, but for a short while I became involved with an actual dance group. This would have been after I had been dancing for a good few years, when I was living in Houston. The Chippendales were at the height of their popularity, and men stripping and doing exotic dancing had moved into the mainstream.

One day this young lady called Latoya who I'd gotten to know through the club scene announced that she was forming a Chippendales-type dance group and she was looking for fit, sexy male dancers to perform in it. She would manage the group and arrange bookings for appearances at clubs and parties, for which she would get a cut of the fees, and she reckoned that everyone involved would make a lot of money. She asked me and two white dancers I knew named Little Red and Exstasey if we would be interested in joining the group. We said we would. We maintained our independence, continuing to dance individually as we had been doing before, but getting together when Latoya booked us a gig.

To start off with my performing name was Mister Wonderful, but later I changed it to The Black Stallion as I was the one black dancer in the group. Even then I was looking for the best way to stand out from the crowd, and being the one among the many was a good start.

We danced for both men and women at various clubs in Houston—Uptown Downtown, Club Incognito, Gremlin, and the Midtown Spa—but on the whole I preferred dancing for men: they were more respectful.

We would do live shows for women at a club called Gremlin, and that was a big eye-opener for me because those women would come on to us like crazy. Being a big, black Mandingo-looking dancer I was extremely popular with the ladies, as you can imagine. Some of the women had their boyfriends there, and of course they were jealous of us. A lot of the women were also very large. Little Red and Exstasey liked that, but I found it a total turn-off. I also found that the women could be extremely aggressive, shrieking drunkenly, groping and clawing at us while we danced, and I didn't like that either. And if they were like that in a club, at a private party they'd be even worse.

It quickly reached the point where when Latoya told me she was lining up work for us I'd ask her, "Latoya, what kind of booking is it?"

"A private dance at a house," she would tell me.

"For one person or what?" I would ask.

"No," she would say guardedly. "A group."

"Of men?"

"No," she'd say. "A group of women."

"Okay," I'd say. "I'll pass."

You can imagine my attitude didn't impress Latoya or the other guys I was supposed to be dancing with, so I quit. It was good money, but I left the group without any regrets, and now I can't even recall its name.

I danced, off and on, for twenty-seven years, and I will always be grateful for the fun times it afforded me, and for the living I earned from it. More important than any of that, though, is the fact that if I hadn't been dancing I might never have met the man with whom I would have the first serious romantic relationship of my life: 'Lou.'

CHAPTER EIGHT:

LOU

Lou was the first serious mate of my life, and we were together for twelve stormy years. He came into one of the bars I was performing at, The Apartment Club, and after I got off the platform he approached me. He was extremely attractive: well-groomed, 5'10", with a great natural physique, a small waistline, big legs—a body to die for. We talked, and found we had a rapport. We didn't have sex that night, though; he went back to his place and I came back home alone. Maybe that's how I knew this relationship was going to be something different.

Lou was five years my junior—I would have been around twenty-three when we met—and came from North Memphis.

Now here's a funny thing—my parents knew I was gay. They knew I was dancing in bars in a g-string. They surely guessed I was having wild sex all over the place. And I could cope with all that. But because they had always brought me up never to have anything to do with anyone from North

Memphis on account of how rough and high-crime it was, my first instinct was to say to myself, "Oh, I couldn't go out with this guy. He's from North Memphis." It sounds crazy, but that's how I felt when Lou first told me where he was from.

A big part of it was surely that I was back living under my parents' roof. Since they had saved me financially, and caught me when all my so-called friends from the bars and clubs would have let me fall, I felt the least I could do was to respect their rules and judgments.

But love finds a way. Lou and I started talking regularly on the phone, and we both realized there was more to our attraction than just sexual desire. Eventually he came over to the house and I introduced him to Mom and Dad. Since he was handsome and polite, and clearly liked me a great deal, they were prepared to forgive him for coming from North Memphis, and two months later Lou and I moved in to our own place together. I gave up dancing for him, and to begin with it was a wonderful relationship.

I also gave up the church I had been attending, and here I have to go back and talk a little about my relationship with the Church and God. Or maybe I should say "relationships" because God and the Church are not the same thing, and can sometimes even be in opposition to each other, so a person can have a good relationship with God and a bad one with the Church, and the other way around.

The congregation of the church at which I am assistant pastor today knows I am bisexual, and they know about my past, and they accept me. Not everyone is so tolerant, of course. But when people condemn me to Hell for my homo-sexuality I don't let it bother me. I believe I have been placed here on Earth to communicate with my Father on a person-al level. Not through the intercession of my pastor, however much I value his preaching. Nor through my bishop, how-ever much I value his guidance. Nor through my fellow-believers, however much I value being surrounded by a sup-portive community of believers. For me the Church is there to provide institutional support for a wholly personal spiri-tual relationship.

My favorite prophet is David because David, as you may recall, had a personal relationship with God. He had friends, he had associates, but he didn't allow them to come between him and God. And this is how I think it should be. Just as you shouldn't allow the people around you to dictate your relationship with your romantic partner, nor should you let them tell you what your relationship with God should be. You need to study the Bible and ask God for guidance, and whatever answer He gives you, be it according to your faith, let your belief be based upon that. Because in the end you have to answer for yourself, and seeking the approval of oth-ers can be a distraction from seeking for what is true for you.

I don't seek to tell others that their beliefs are wrong; if they believe homosexuality is a sin, so be it. That is their belief. I don't share it, but I don't have an agenda to promote, either spiritual, social, or political. But nor do I tolerate others telling me that my beliefs are wrong: that is between me and God.

Now, my foster-mother raised me a Methodist. I

attended the Methodist chapel when I was at Tennessee Preparatory School, and when I moved in with my adoptive parents I continued to be active in the Methodist church. At the age of sixteen, shortly after my foster-mother's passing, I began to feel a calling to the ministry. A year or so later, by which time I was living with my adoptive parents, I was taken before the church board and put on trial. This means that I was questioned about the sincerity and intensity of my sense of vocation. A year after that I was given my license as a local minister in the Methodist church. This meant I could preach, carry out duties around the church, and do outreach work of various sorts, though I was not yet ordained.

At the same time as I was pursuing my calling in the church I was feeling the pull of the world of the flesh, the gay world. In fact, throughout my life you could plot a graph which would show that when I was most strongly involved in one I was most withdrawn from the other.

It would be easy to say that these two aspects of my life were in opposition to each other, as if the Church was Heaven, the gay clubs and bars Hell, but in reality they were more like oil and water: to me they simply didn't mix. And more important than whether I was living my life in a church or a night-club is that I continued to maintain a strong spiritual relationship with the God of Abraham, Isaac, and Jacob in whom I never ceased to believe. My faith never wavered, except for one single time. But that is the subject of a later chapter.

When Lou and I met I had pulled back from taking a prominent role at my church; I had begun stripping and platform-dancing at gay bars for money as well as just for fun, and it didn't feel right to be doing that and preaching at the same time.

Lou was inclined to be jealous. I guess most men would be uneasy about having their mate display his all-but-naked body to the eager gaze of other men in some packed gay bar, so I understood why he felt that way, and I quit dancing. Truth to tell I was bored of it by then anyway, and welcomed a break from a nightly grind that had become as routine as any other job.

Like me, Lou was a keen churchgoer. He and his family were Baptists, and they attended a church I'll call Greater Mount Pleasant in North Memphis. Somewhat weary of the gay world, and finding myself in a stable loving relationship, I guess it was natural that my pastoral side would reassert itself around that time. Lou invited me to start attending his church, and I was pleased to do so.

It was made easy for me because Lou's family knew he was gay and knew about our relationship. They were very supportive of both him and us, and even today his family and my family are close. The members of the Greater Mount Pleasant congregation were friendly and welcoming, and were in the main very accepting of the fact that Lou and I were mates, with two exceptions who I'll get to in a moment.

The Methodist and Baptist churches are quite different from one another. The Methodist church is more conservative in that the rules are more clearly laid down and consistently abided by. In the Methodist church the bishop ordains and appoints the pastor. In the Baptist church the members vote on the pastorship, and there is more room for each congregation to set its own rules and decide on how it wants to do things. I prefer the Methodist church because I prefer clear rules, discipline, and a well-ordered hierarchy, but I joined Greater Mount Pleasant because it was an opportunity for me to throw myself into new challenges and grow as a person.

The pastor was an older man deeply rooted in his own ways. He ran another church as well as Greater Mount Pleasant, but his health was failing and he was finding it increasingly hard to keep up with his duties in either of his churches. He didn't want to officially step down as pastor, but it was clear he needed an assistant at each church to keep things going.

I was very active in Greater Mount Pleasant by that point, and was particularly concerned with supporting young people. Having quit stripping, to pay my way I had taken a job working as a fast food manager at Krystal's restaurant, and I would hire some of the young people from the church to work at the restaurant, thereby helping them to help themselves. My belief is, if you're going to ask your congregation to pay tithes then the least you can do is help them get the jobs to earn the money to be able to pay the tithes. A ministry should be about the whole well-being of the congregation, and not just stop at the church door.

It may surprise you, given the reputation the "Black Church" has for homophobia, that most of the congregation accepted that Lou and I were lovers, but I think a large part of it is down to how you carry yourself. I have always carried myself in a way that demands respect from anyone I meet. I'm always careful to show respect to others, and so I have been respected in return.

So I didn't feel in any way awkward about putting myself forward for the role of intern, that is, assistant pastor, at Greater Mount Pleasant.

The pastor, however, was a traditionalist. He disapproved of homosexuality, wouldn't embrace gay people, and, despite my good works with the church's young folks and my dedication to Greater Mount Pleasant, was somewhat obstructive. Since I had been an intern at my previous church, he could have simply accepted me in the role. Instead he said I would have to be elected by the congregation.

I had no reason to object, so I said, "Of course."

I had assumed I would be elected without any controversy, but at one point during the election process one of the mothers of the church stood up and said, "Reverend, you shouldn't take this position."

I was shocked because Lou and I had done a lot to help this lady and her family through some difficult times, with counseling, advice, and helping some of the younger family members to get jobs.

"You shouldn't take this job because that's your lover sitting there right beside you," she continued, jabbing a finger in Lou's direction.

The old me would have been combative and said something cutting in return, but all of a sudden I don't know what happened because not a word would come out of my mouth. I just didn't know what to say. Awkward silence yawned. And then to my delight and great relief other members of the congregation began to stir and come to my defense. They told this homophobic lady, "That's not your business. You need to be quiet because everyone knows your husband has a child that's not yours."

From which I conclude: if you treat people right, if you respect folks, then God always helps folks to step up on your behalf.

I was elected assistant pastor, and although the old pastor was somewhat grudging in his support of me, because I had the backing of the congregation, and because I had been running services on his behalf anyway every other Sunday while he was at his other church, I was able to immediately set to getting the church in better order. I brought in the more disciplined mindset of the Methodist church. I strove to instill the mentality that it's important to not only get across the preaching—the proclaiming of the Gospel—but the teaching; that is, the explaining of the Gospel.

The role of intern is a salaried position, and I brought in financial reforms and insisted on appointing an administrator to take of the business side of things. It was hard work and extremely draining because people were set in their ways, but it was also very rewarding and the people *shone*. I was so proud of them and what they achieved.

During the year and a half I was assistant pastor at Greater Mount Pleasant our congregation grew from maybe eighty people to around seven hundred. Our income grew considerably, and today Greater Mount Pleasant has moved to a new church that cost over a million dollars. I still visit occasionally and the people over there treat me real nice. I'm very proud to have been part of that development, building on the work the old pastor had done, and passing on what I had done to my successor.

It was a very successful ministry, but after a year and a half I found myself missing the structure and discipline of the Methodist church. Also, I felt that I had done what I had been brought to do at Greater Mount Pleasant. I felt a certain restlessness and a desire to be free from the obligations of being a minister. I got a friend to come across from his church and take over running the church for me, and I stepped down.

By this time Lou and I had taken the step of buying a house together over in East Memphis, in a well-to-do middle-class area. Before that we were renting in North Memphis. The house we were renting was on North Main Street, and it backed onto a wooded area. After night fell cars would pull in back there and park under the spreading branches of the trees, it was a place for sexual assignations.

Some summer evenings we would put out the lights and watch couples having sex by moonlight: guys and girls, guys and guys, none of them knowing we were watching them. It was kind of unbelievable to just sit there in the dark and see it all going on. When the moon was full it was almost as bright as day, and sometimes the breeze would carry the sounds of their passion to our ears.

But most of the time we lived quiet, regular lives, Lou and I. He was a good cook, we both worked hard in regular jobs, we were very loyal to each other, and for the first two, maybe three years we were very happy together, confident enough in each other in fact to decide to take the plunge and commit to buying a house together.

If it hadn't been for the drinking we might still be together today.

CHAPTER NINE:

THE BOTTLE

Because of my strict upbringing I have never drunk alcohol. Despite working in gay bars and clubs I have never drunk, smoked cigarettes, or used drugs. I guess Lou had always been a big drinker, but when we first became involved he saw that I wouldn't accept a partner who drank heavily, and he hid his taste for alcohol from me. There were probably signs that I missed since I hadn't been brought up around people who drank, but over time his drinking became more and more obvious. He began to drink more and more heavily and his conduct deteriorated until finally I was confronted with the inescapable fact that my mate was an alcoholic.

Now he lives in Dallas. He's not drinking and I hear he has a new partner, and I'm glad. I count him as a friend, and I'm proud of what he's achieved with his life. But back then we went through some extremely tough times, and I did things I thought I would never be capable of doing.

I blame the failure of our relationship on alcohol, but of course it's more complicated than that. I can't blame Lou for

everything that went wrong; I couldn't deal with his problems, and I was young and headstrong. But I did my best.

Although I had given up dancing, I was highly sociable
and I still enjoyed going to gay bars and clubs. Of course
guys would come on to me, and that would drive Lou wild
with jealousy even though I wasn't looking to do anything
with them. He would insist on coming out with me, to keep
an eye on me, then he would get drunk and either nod off
on his barstool or in the corner of some club, or he would
provoke a row with me or a fight with some guy who had
been flirting with me. And because his behavior angered and
upset me, I would want to get out of the house more and
more. And the more I was out of the house, the more he
drank and the crazier his behavior became. He would fall
asleep at the wheel of his car, get in car wrecks, and one time
he even ran a couple down.

It happened this way: we were visiting his mom over in
North Memphis. She was a beautiful woman, a caring, loving mother, very down-to-earth, and she attended the same
church we did. She was a very good cook, and we had just
enjoyed a fine meal, but Lou was drunk yet again, and he
and I had a heated argument right on the porch of his mother's house. He stormed off, got behind the wheel of his car,
slammed the door, started the engine and pulled out fast
without due care and attention. He hit a couple who happened to be crossing the street at that moment and sent them
tumbling right over the hood of his car and sprawling on the
asphalt.

He pulled up, confused and frightened, and his mom and

I came down the steps. She was a very sharp lady, and I guess she knew that this couple was nothing but a pair of drunks themselves, because she picked 'em up and dusted 'em off. "Y'all okay?" she asked them, and before they had a chance to answer she added, "Y'all want a bottle? I'll buy you something at the liquor store." The liquor store was just across the street, and she reckoned if she got them full enough of alcohol they wouldn't be together enough to file a report.

They nodded and she pushed twenty dollars into their hands and sent them on their way, and they never did report anything.

It seemed like they had just been bruised and shaken, but I had to laugh when I saw that same couple two days later: the woman had a cast on her arm and the man was on crutches. They had sobered up too late to do anything about it.

My relationship with Lou started to go downhill fast. As is so often the case with extremely jealous people, Lou started cheating on me.

I remember waking up one night in the small hours and finding myself alone in our bed. He had been out with friends, and hadn't yet come back. I had a strange feeling; something told me to go back to where we used to live on Main Street. I don't know what it was, but I acted on it I drove over to Main Street. I parked the car out front and snuck round the back to the wooded area where the courting couples went to make out.

There was Lou's green Malibu, parked there.

I snuck up to it. The glass was fogged but I could see Lou

was in there with another guy. I was so mad I took my fist and I knocked the glass out with a punch that cut my knuckles and almost broke my hand, and I tried to grab him. He freaked out, started up the motor, threw the car into drive and I jumped back out of harm's way as he slammed his foot down on the accelerator. But in his panic he'd jammed the gear-stick into reverse, and he sent the car speeding backwards into a ditch with him and the other guy in it. As I watched the front end of it tip up I felt I'd made my point, so I melted away into the dark, leaving him to sort himself out.

You can believe he was scared to come home that night.

He hadn't learned his lesson, though. I woke up another night to find him gone again.

In downtown Memphis there used to be an area called the Ho Track, which was where all the hustler boys hung out, and guys would go there to have a trashy time. It's been redeveloped since, and is now the site of the Red Birds' stadium. As before, for some reason I had a strong feeling that that was where I would find Lou. I got my gun and I got in my car and I drove down there.

I saw Lou's car and I pulled up behind it. This young guy was sitting on the passenger side next to Lou. I went round to the passenger side, leaned in through the open window, and said to the boy, "Do you know this guy?"

"No," he said. He was nervous and ready to run.

"Then why are you in his car?" I asked.

"Well, he just picked me up," he said.

That was all I needed to hear. I walked round to Lou's side

of the car. He was just sitting there, not saying anything, not doing anything, staring ahead. I showed him the gun. I pointed it towards his head and said, "I should kill you. But I'm not going to." And I got back in my car and I drove back home. And as soon as I got in the door, boom! All my feelings for him just left. Just like that.

It's strange when that happens. In one way it's liberating, in another it's scary: that love can vanish at the snap of a switch.

After that I didn't care who Lou had sex with. To prove that to myself I even paid a guy to have sex with him. I paid a guy to fuck my mate and I felt nothing. And to prove to Lou that I no longer cared for him, after they'd fucked I told him what I had done.

We continued to live together, but we slept in separate rooms; we were no longer a couple.

Perversely enough, Lou became more jealous after the relationship had broken down than he had been before. And I have to admit I gave him cause, although by then I didn't feel he had the right to be jealous, what with all the running around he'd been doing behind my back.

I had a friend I'll call 'Dee'. He and I would go off and do things we shouldn't do. We would go down to the Ho Track and mess with the guys and generally act like whores. One evening we picked up this guy and took him down a dark alley for some fun. And both of us, we were just fucking this guy from both ends and all of a sudden the lights came on in a house that overlooked the alley. We paused for a moment in what we were doing. Then, when we didn't see anybody come out, we just carried on fucking. And then all of a sudden somebody came running out of the house, yelling, "What you motherfuckers doin'?"

We ran as best we could, stumbling as we pulled up our pants, breathless and laughing and scared.

Lou and I were living in the shell of a relationship. Our situation hit rock-bottom one Saturday evening when he invited me to go out with him and a buddy of his up to Beale Street. This would have been shortly before I left Greater Mount Pleasant. I was preaching the next morning and had a sermon to prepare so I said I had better stay in and get that done. Of course he and his buddy got seriously drunk, and when he finally staggered home in the small hours, Lou accused me of having had someone over to the house in his absence and fucked him. It was drunken paranoia, and it made me extremely angry. I denied his accusation and he picked up the telephone, ripped it out of the wall-socket and threw it at me real hard. It hit me on the head and cut my scalp open.

At the sight of my blood the storm of his rage blew out. He started crying and trying to apologize. Ignoring his drunken whining I clapped a cloth to my bleeding head and left the house. The cut was sufficiently long and deep enough for me to know it would require stitches. As I drove myself to the hospital all I could think was that I was going to have to stand up in front of the congregation the next morning and preach with a gash on my head—which by now I always kept shaved—caused by my alcoholic boyfriend throwing a phone at me.

To my relief the doctor did a good job; I didn't need too many stitches, and the end result didn't stand out too much.

I drove home. I didn't say a word to Lou. I showered and changed, then went to church. I preached my sermon. It was titled, appropriately enough, "What to do in the middle of a storm," although perhaps it wasn't the time for me to be telling anyone else what they should do in the face of personal difficulties. *[handwritten annotation: This is what the epitome of christian behaviour all about. Doesn't make any sense]*

I came home. Lou was there, wanting to talk. I didn't say a word. I just went and got a heavy stick from the yard and I took it and I broke both his arms. I broke both his arms in *[handwritten annotation: How can any believer take him seriously speaks to this simple minds by how to deal with]* two or three places, and I told him, "Nobody's going to be beating on me. I didn't hit on you. You have to find another way to handle your drinking."

First off, Lou went down to Saint Joseph's hospital and ridiculously enough they told him there was nothing wrong with his arms, so to this day that's a hospital I would never go to. Since he was still in a lot of pain he went to another hospital, the Regional Medical Center, where I worked as a chaplain. There they x-rayed him and that's when he learned that I had broken each of his arms in two or three places. They put his arms in plaster and he had to get a cab home because he couldn't drive like that. When he got home he couldn't feed himself, so I fed him. I took care of him until the casts came off.

Now, my foster-mother didn't raise me to be a violent person, but on the other hand I'm not going to allow you to do me any harm. I don't hit you, I don't bother you, but if you bother me then you've made your choice.

I'm not a violent person, but my relationship with Lou was driving me to violence. One time I got so furious with him that I dragged him out of his mom's house and whipped him right out in the street in front of his mom and his family. I was so mad I told them, "Don't none of y'all move!" Because he had done something that had enraged me. I forget what. It might have been serious or it might have been extremely trivial; by that point I had a temper I could barely keep control of.

I guess the arm-breaking was the incident that made me realize that I wasn't being the person I was raised to be, and I wasn't being the person I wanted to be. I decided I had to formally end our relationship before I hurt Lou even more. It was after that that I insisted on separate bedrooms. I never made any bones about bringing guys back to our home, and I told Lou that he could do the same. I was done with him. It took him a while to accept that and adjust to our new living arrangements, but eventually he came round to it and we began to build a friendship out of the rubble of what had gone before. We continued to share the house we were buying together for the next eight or so years, although for much of that time I was living in other cities: Houston, Oakland, and Los Angeles. No doubt it helped him cope with the new situation that at the same time as I was away so much I was still paying half the mortgage.

CHAPTER TEN:

TROUBLING THE WATER

During my difficult times with Lou I would often pray to God and ask Him for guidance. He gave me the strength to keep on moving forward with my life when it would have been easy to go off the rails altogether.

Yet my relationship with the Church, which should be God's house and His instrument, was ambivalent. This was entirely due to the Church's attitude towards homosexuality.

On the one hand every week preachers and pastors were stepping up to their pulpits to denounce homosexuality as if it was the only so-called sin there is.

On the other hand I was having certain experiences that convinced me that many of these preachers were indulging in private in the very activities they condemned so aggressively in public.

One time I was invited to a party along with two friends of mine, 'Joseph' and 'Karl'. This is while I was still assistant pastor at Greater Mount Pleasant. We arrived at the address and knocked on the door. It was an apartment in a well-to-do part of Memphis. The host opened the door to welcome us in. From the doorway we could see straight through to the lounge and there were a number of other guys sitting around in there, all of 'em naked as the day they was born. And sitting there among them was a preacher I knew, a man who led a sizeable congregation, which is how come I recognized him.

Well, the guys weren't really our type physically, so we kind of drew back, Joseph, Karl, and myself. The guy whose party it was tried to grab me by my coat.

"C'mon in," he said.

"Naw, man," I said. "I'm gon' go. Shit." He tried to pull me in and I said, "Man, if you don't let me go I'll have to just knock you out."

Well, he took his hand off me and we left. But you can believe me when I tell you that bare-ass naked preacher would be up in his pulpit come Sunday, thundering on 'bout Leviticus and abominations.

Another time I had an encounter with a minister whose installation service I had attended. He was tall, maybe 6'1", a beautiful light-skinned man, and I had a crush on him. I remember thinking to myself as I watched his wife escort him up the aisle, "That bitch ought to be out of the way. That should be me escorting him in, not her."

I shouldn't have shamed myself that way in church, but right then I said to myself, "I'm gon' have him."

Now, that was nothing but the devil in me. I didn't mean

nothing by it, and I didn't intend to do anything about it. But one day about a month later I was at the YMCA, working out. Once I finished working out I went in the steam room to unwind and there this minister was, naked.

You don't have nothing but a towel around you when you go in the steam room, and some of the guys would take off their towels and sit on them so their butts didn't get burnt by the hot boards. This is what he had done, and I noticed that he was eyeing me and getting a hard-on. There was only the two of us in there, and my dick started getting hard too.

The door into the steam room had a little window in it, and he got up and went and looked out of the window to see if anybody was coming. I stood and pretended like I was going out the door, and as I was standing by the door I brushed up against his ass. He let out a soft groan.

Well, the steam room was too public for both of us, so I ended up taking him home and fucking him there. And while I was fucking this beautiful man I thought how amazing it was that only a month ago I had attended his installation service and watched him standing there with his wife at his side, envying her.

Though I never abandoned God, these kinds of things pushed me away from the Church. And they added to my growing impression that most men are dogs.

CHAPTER ELEVEN:

TRAVELLIN'
LIGHT

The disastrous and traumatic way my relationship with Lou had broken down left me cynical and self-protective when it came to matters of the heart, and it's no accident that my next few involvements were shallow. Nor should it come as any surprise that I felt a desire to get out of Memphis for a while and become someone new in a new city.

Houston was to be that city, and I was to live there for the next three years.

This is the story of how I came to be in Houston. A good friend of mine named 'Derek' knew Lou and I had broken up. I had quit my job as a fast-food manager at Krystal's by then and had gone back to dancing, and I would perform not only in Memphis, but also I did shows regularly in Birmingham, Atlanta, and Houston.

One time when I was in Houston I went to the Texas

relays and met a lot of track-stars. They were all over me, these supposed straight guys, and I wound up visiting some of them at their homes and hanging out with them, having fun. That led to me having a very favorable impression of Houston. So when Derek told me that he knew somebody in Houston who had totally fallen in love with me—or rather, with my physical appearance—I was intrigued. Derek gave me his phone number and I called him up and we got talking. His name was 'Hall'. We hit it off big time and pretty soon I was talking to him up to three times a day.

Needless to say our talk had a flirtatious and sexual element.

Now, I've always been an extremely upfront person about what I like and don't like sexually, and in the course of our conversations I let Hall know early on that I don't like heavy guys who are just plain fat. Now, don't be offended when you hear me saying that, because we all have choices. We all have things we prefer and things we don't prefer. Everybody don't like big, black, bald-headed men, and I accept that. Everybody don't like black men, everybody don't like tall men or small men or what have you. We all have choices, and just because someone doesn't like me sexually doesn't mean he or she doesn't like me as a person, and it doesn't mean that I'm unattractive to people in general. [My sense of myself doesn't rely on what you think of me, and nor should yours rely on what I think of you.] *That's an adult perspective. I've children are shaped*

To me overweight-ness and unfit-ness, apart from being unattractive in themselves, represent self-indulgence, self-

by others opinions this u why we have to be careful that we teach them not undermining their self-continue but neither giving them false esteem.

neglect, and a lack of self-love, and I find it hard to believe that someone who doesn't love himself will be able to love someone else.

So there I was talking to Hall two, three times a day, and every morning he would say, "I gotta go now, I'm on my way to my aerobics class." So naturally I thought, "Hey, this guy's got to be in good shape."

I enjoyed talking with him, we seemed to get along pretty well, and after a while he invited me to come stay with him in Houston. I had nothing tying me to Memphis at that time, and the idea of getting away from the house I was still living in with Lou made his offer all the more attractive. So I said, "Sure I'll come visit you. Why not?"

"I'll buy you a ticket and you can fly out," Hall said.

"Make it a round-trip ticket," I said.

By then I was smart enough to make sure I never got trapped in any situation however broke I might find myself.

Hall bought me a one month round-trip ticket.

I flew to Houston that weekend. After I'd touched down and collected my baggage I got out my cell-phone and called Hall to tell him I was in Arrivals waiting for him. He answered and said, "I'm coming across the parking lot right now." I looked round and *damn*, that guy was fat! Not just heavy: *obese*. Wheezing as he walked.

Well, I played it off. We carried my bags to his car and he drove us back to his apartment. All the time I'm not saying much, and he can tell something's wrong. When we got back to his place I'd hardly had time to put my bags down in the hall before he put the moves on me. He wanted to lay down with me, have sex with me right then and there.

"Hold on," I said. "You don't know me. For all you know I could have AIDS."

I knew that would be a passion-killer because this was way before anyone had come up with anti-retrovirals and combination therapies, and AIDS was still a death sentence. "You can't just jump on me like that," I went on. "Let's get to know each other first and then we'll see."

I knew I wasn't going to let nothing happen but I didn't feel guilty about what I was saying because it was Hall who had lied to me in the first place.

I stayed in Hall's apartment as we had agreed but mostly I ignored him. I found out where the clubs were at and made friends and started having some fun. I danced, sometimes five nights a week, and made good money at it—I could earn five hundred dollars a night or more—and so I was able to be independent of Hall and keep up my share of the mortgage back in Memphis.

I carried on like that until my month was almost up, and it was the day before I was due to fly back home.

Hall was a messy kind of queen. He had four or five lines on one phone, and sometimes he would be talking to one person on one line not realizing that another person would be listening in on one of the other lines. He was psychologically messy in that way.

Now, Hall had a friend who was a doctor, and several times he told me the story of how this doctor had bought his ex-lover a car, thinking that I would be impressed by the story in itself, and that I would be impressed with him for having such an extravagant buddy. The doctor's name was 'Charles'.

I was looking at my unpacked bags, feeling no particular desire to go back to Memphis, and Hall was in the other room, talking to Charles on the phone. They weren't talking about anything in particular, but suddenly an idea popped into my head.

I waited until Hall had gone to work—by then we were barely speaking to each other—and I pushed redial on the phone, and I hit Charles up and started talking to him. I'd guessed—rightly—that just as Hall had bragged to me about Charles's generosity, he had bragged to his doctor friend about the hot stud he had living with him.

"Hall's out," I said. "Why don't you come on over?"

Charles jumped at the chance.

Now, I'm not saying all men are dogs, just most of 'em. And of course I knew exactly what I was doing. I pulled on some cycling shorts and lifted some weights to pump myself up to the max, and I put some oil on my chest and arms and legs. I was on a mission. When he came to the door and he saw me he said, "Damn!"

I'd taken a chance because I'd never met Charles, and I might have found him as unattractive as Hall, but my first thought when I saw him was that he was a hot guy himself. I invited him in and he asked me, "When are you leaving? Let me see that ticket." I showed it to him and he took it off me and tore it up right in front of my face.

"What the hell are you doing?" I said angrily. "I'm leaving tomorrow!"

"No, you're not," he said. "We'll get you another ticket when you're ready to go home. Get your bags."

And I got my bags, and I left.

Such a sudden change of circumstances was exhilarating. But not for long. I was out of Hall's apartment, which was a relief, but right away I was in another complicated situation because Charles was dating a woman schoolteacher. There I was, living in his house with him, and he had this girlfriend who would come over regularly, and whom he was planning to marry. I don't know if she guessed what was going on between us, but she certainly didn't like me being around.

Charles treated me well. He took care of me, put me up and generally did everything I wanted to do. But he was very much on the down-low, and that could be extremely irritating and tedious because he wanted to both hide me and have me.

For instance, we would fly down to visit his mom in Dallas. He would insist I come with him, and would pay to put me up in a hotel. He would stay with his mom, and then sneak out of her house and come and see me. In one way that was fine; I don't demand that my mate announce his sexuality to the world. But he was also the kind of guy who always wants to be around you, hugging and kissing all the time, and I don't like a lot of that kind of attention. My attitude was: we can have all the fun you like, then you go to your space, go to your girlfriend, go to your mom, go do what it is you have to do, and I'll do what I want to do. I can be quite happy with that kind of emotionally low-key situation. But the combination of the furtiveness and concealment with clingy, over-attentiveness was just claustrophobic.

As a consequence of all that my situation with Charles didn't last much longer than the one I'd been in with Hall; just about a month or so. After that I simplified things and moved in with a buddy I'd made in Houston by then named 'Trevone', and we shared an apartment for nearly two years.

We weren't in a relationship, me and Trevone. We were just friends, but our friendship deepened over those two years, and we're still the best of friends today, and talk on the phone practically every day. It was Trevone who showed me the ropes when I first came to Houston, and all the time I was there he looked out for me.

It was during that time that I joined the dance group and performed all over the South. It was another of my wilder times and, just like before, a time came when I had done enough and seen enough. I became bored with it and I felt home calling. I was missing friends and above all I was missing family.

I flew back to Memphis and moved back into the house I had bought with Lou. He was still living in it. By then we had worked our way through to a genuine friendship, the friendship which can only exist between two people who are bound together by the hard times they have been through with each other.

I quit dancing and started becoming more involved with the church. I was back in the Methodist fold, though I didn't rejoin my former church; it would have felt like going backwards in my life.

To pay the bills I found myself a job cutting meat as a

butcher, which I enjoyed. I'm a people person and I like any job which gives me a chance to talk with people, and it was a sociable place to work. I was hard-working when I was actually there, but I can't say I was a model employee because I would refuse to work weekends because that's when I would be out having a good time. That would have been okay with my bosses, but I never used to come to work on Mondays either, for the same reason. It used to drive Jack and Gary, the head butcher and the head manager, crazy. Jack would challenge me when I hadn't shown up for the tenth time and I'd just laugh and say, "Well, you ought to be used to it by now!"

My secret for not getting fired from that job was that whenever I had to train up a new staff member I'd always show them the wrong way to do things. Never let anybody know your job better than you do! That kept Jack and Gary relying on me, and that was how I liked it. I was smart, and I was in control. Also—and this is important to notice—I did work real hard when I was there, and I was popular with the other members of staff.

Everyone I worked with in the meat department knew I was bisexual because sometimes Lou would come by the store. Now, Lou didn't look gay, but there must have been something in the way we related to each other physically because one time, early on, someone asked me right in front of everybody else in the department, "Is that your boyfriend?"

Expecting me to deny it, you know?

"No," I said. "He's my ex."

That got a big laugh from the rest of the staff, and from then on my sexuality didn't seem to bother anyone. Because I carried myself in a masculine way and never came on to anyone they weren't threatened or offended by my preference.

My job as a butcher ended when I got injured using a forklift truck. I had left the engine running, and I guess I must have left it in gear. I was round the front of it straightening the load on a palette that hadn't been properly secured when the damn truck jumped forward and pinned me against the wall. One of the forks stuck straight into my thigh, which was alarming and extremely painful.

Fortunately there were people around to help me. They got the truck backed up and called an ambulance. I had to go to the hospital and have surgery on my leg. The wound was nasty, but no bones were broken, and today you wouldn't even be able to see the scar. But I had to take some time off, and after that I didn't want to go back to butchering.

Instead I went into fast food management, something I'd done briefly before going to Houston. It turned out I had an aptitude. Although I didn't have degrees or formal qualifications, I was smart enough to go on the job, work hard, learn the procedures, and rise to the top. That's something I've always managed to do wherever I've worked, even at the butcher's I was the supervisor. With fast food management I went from regular employee to shift manager to assistant manager.

I've always believed that if you want to accomplish something you can; if you work hard enough you can become the

utter rubbish! Only parroting the anodyne nonsense
which keeps the poor in permanent expectation.

manager, the owner, whatever you want to be.

Krystal's was probably the most rewarding of the chains I worked for. When I joined the particular outlet I worked at there was a real negative atmosphere, and I managed to turn it around and the staff appreciated me for doing that. We were like one big, happy family. They knew about me, too, because male as well as female customers would flirt with me and the other employees would see me flirt back.

It was also during the tail-end of my relationship with Lou, when he was still being mad-jealous and would turn up at my workplace to check up on me. Because he was so good-looking the girls would be envious. They would see me and Lou together and laugh and say, "Damn, we can't even get a man because of you! Every damn man come up here want to talk to you!"

So we would have fun, me and the girls. Most of them had kids and I would help them look out for their kids and help them get promoted. I never had any problems with anyone, not even with the guys. I respected them and their sexuality. I never came on to any of them. I think we as a society have to understand that you can't just go around coming on to folks, men or women. You shouldn't disrespect people. Life is all about respecting people, and if you respect them they respect you in return. And that's how it was at Krystal's.

Having risen to management level in Krystal's before going off to Houston, after quitting the butcher's I managed a Taco Bell and then a Jack Pirtle's. I worked as a fast-food manager for a couple of years and always did a good job, but I got tired of it. It didn't pay that well, and while it was great working with good people, which most of the time I was, it was the kind of job you take home with you.

I felt my life was stagnating.

I did have one romance during this time, with a guy I met named 'Walter'. I was still living with Lou, but it wasn't too awkward because Walter had his own place out east; he had a condo he shared with a roommate, and mostly I would go there. I spent a lot of time with him. He worked at the university. We both loved tennis and we would go to one of the courts on campus and play almost every day. I was in love with Walter.

We got along real well, we had this great relationship, it seemed, but after a while I realized Walter didn't love me as much as I loved him. And he wasn't as faithful as I'd thought he would be, I caught him a couple of times with other guys. That changed things between us. Strangely enough it didn't break my heart. It just made me realize that Walter and I worked better as friends than lovers. And it reminded me that sex and love are very different things: you can have passionate sex with someone while being emotionally lukewarm towards them.

We decided to be friends, but agreed that just because we were no longer lovers it didn't mean that we couldn't still have sex. And we did. Several times we did threesomes, and that was fun, but it was nothing to do with love.

It was shortly after that relationship fizzled out that I met my second real mate and the love of my life: 'Jermaine'.

CHAPTER TWELVE:

YOU DON'T REMEMBER ME

Jack Pirtle's had gone bust, so I was out of a job, foot-loose, and fancy-free. I was in Atlanta for Gay Pride weekend. It was a hot, sunny day, the sky was blue, and I was out in Piedmont Park just kicking back and enjoying the general scene with some friends. I recall some guy trying to talk to me, but I didn't give him the time of day. I didn't pay him any real attention; my impression was that he wasn't as masculine a man as I was looking for, so I brushed him off and just carried on talking with my friends, thinking nothing of it.

That night I was at a club called Bulldogs and I saw this gorgeous, gorgeous boy. He was 5'10", maybe 140 pounds, extremely well-groomed with close-cut hair, had a beautiful face, a great ass, and a flawless physique. We talked a little and I gave him my number at the hotel I was staying at. His name was Jermaine.

The next day he called me at the hotel and I invited him over. When he arrived the first thing he said to me was, "You don't remember me."

"Yeah, I do," I said. "I saw you at Bulldogs. I gave you my number."

"You saw me even before that," he said.

"What do you mean?"

"I'm the guy you gave the brush-off to in the park."

"You couldn't be!" I said. But he was. I was shocked. Maybe it was that he had adopted a more flamboyant style of dressing in the park; certainly he had a more masculine style when I met him in the club. But whatever the reason, I didn't care, I had come to Atlanta for a weekend adventure, Jermaine was gorgeous, and I took him to bed.

We had sex and it was hot. I was wearing his ass out for four hours straight; it was just unbelievable. Just great sex.

Well, that weekend adventure turned into a three-year journey! I didn't go back to Memphis until three years later. We became lovers. And I think I can honestly say that out of all the relationships I have been in, I was truly in love with Jermaine. I love him even today. He was the love of my life and he was my mate. But the relationship failed, and after three years we broke up and I returned to Memphis.

I remember that final journey, flying back home on the plane, heavy with a sense of failure and grieving. Boys II Men had a song out called "When Can I See You Again?" and as I sat there on that plane that song was playing over and over in my head. And because I knew the answer was "never" I started crying and I just couldn't stop.

I didn't care who saw me.

Back in Memphis I tried to get myself together, physically at least. I was in the YMCA in downtown Memphis a few weeks later, working out, when that song came on the radio. Well, I just dropped the weights and walked out; I knew I would start crying and all of a sudden I couldn't face working out any more.

Of all my lovers, Jermaine is the only one I would have back. He's the only one who makes me wish I could turn back time and do it right. *Ok he does admit he been Jami M 70 pm b. 1.79.*

To begin with we had a wonderful relationship. Jermaine was a great cook and a caring, loving mate. We had a beautiful home, a condo in the Druid Hill-Beauford Highway area of Atlanta, which was then an upscale area, quite racially-mixed, although it was to become even more upscale once it was redeveloped. The condo was his, and I moved in with him.

One time I became quite seriously ill; I was passing protein in my urine, which is indicative of kidney problems that can be life-threatening. Thank God I had insurance, because I had to go into a hospital and have a biopsy. Mercifully it proved not to be cancerous, and the doctors sorted the problem out, but it was a frightening time for me, and throughout it Jermaine was a true mate. He made sure the medical staff were doing what they needed to do. He kept my family in Memphis informed. And when I came home from the hospital he looked after me.

I had the privilege of meeting his mother. She's a great woman and I love her to death. She lives in South Carolina, which is where all of Jermaine's family is from. I went down there with him to stay with her one Christmas, and she and his aunt cooked cakes and pies and fried chicken, and there was food for *days*.

Jermaine was an office-worker type guy, a computer technician, and although he was younger than me he had a more settled nature. Even then I was still caught up in the urge to run around and have fun, and here I have to put my hand on my heart and confess that it was my fault that our relationship didn't go the way it should have.

Also, I was still dancing.

It was how I was earning a living, but Jermaine wanted me to give it up and move into a different career. He wanted me to himself. He couldn't take all the attention I was getting when I danced, and I understood that. But as much as I loved him, I refused. I refused because, while I knew he loved me, I felt a deep need for him to accept me as I was without putting limitations on me, and what I was was a dancer. I didn't want to be caged by a regular job again; I had had three years of that in Memphis, and it had taken me nowhere.

So we broke each other's hearts, and it ended. Even today I still love him. We are still regularly in touch, and I'm grateful that we built a loving friendship from a painful break-up. Life is all lessons, and some mistakes you have to make yourself—no amount of advice will save you from them. But I'm grateful that Jermaine found it in himself to forgive me for being so young and foolish at a time when he was both younger and wiser.

I lit out for the West Coast, for something new.

Difficult to fathom whether his acceptance of one was even if he was "young & foolish." How come the same acceptance of unconditional love rec'd from his foster-mother & adoptive parents didn't filter through to these relationships. Why would it be so difficult for him to see that one requires some surrender & [illegible] would have been a small one [illegible] the [illegible] real rewards were really that great

CHAPTER THIRTEEN:

I REACH THE WEST COAST: OAKLAND, CALIFORNIA

If it seems like I was gradually working my way over to Los Angeles, the capital of the adult entertainment industry, I have to say that would be an illusion—my life at that time was much more haphazard and capricious. If God had a plan for me, if He had mapped out a journey for me to follow, I wasn't at that time aware of it. But certainly it was because I was living so much closer to L. A. that I began to go there on a regular basis, and it was on one of those visits that I was given my first chance to perform in an adult film.

Oakland is a predominantly African-American city just across the bay from the more prosperous, picturesque and famous San Francisco. While San Francisco was an early center of the white counter-culture—the Beats, flower power, and gay activism—Oakland was, famously, the birthplace of the Black Panthers, led by Huey P. Newton and Bobby Seale, whose black power salute was to become known across the world. Assata Shakur, Tupac Shakur's aunt, was a member of the group. Imprisoned, she broke jail and fled to Cuba, and the rest of the Panthers were destroyed by government infiltrators, rivals such as Ron Karenga's US, (as in "Us against Them"), paranoia, and drugs.

By the time I reached Oakland, which was in the early Nineties, not only was crack and other drug abuse a huge problem, but AIDS was laying waste to whole swathes of the community. It's hard now to recall the despair of those times when no drug worked and nothing but a genetic lottery determined how long a person could be HIV+ before developing full-blown AIDS and dying in horrible, shrunken agony. AZT was the only drug there was, and it was both lethally toxic and totally ineffective until the sufferer was already so ill that the drug in and of itself would shorten his or her life.

The Republican government, backed by Christian right-wing fundamentalists—including many in the black churches—was quick to lay blame and divide those with the disease into "victims" (such as those infected via contaminated blood transfusions) and "plague-carriers" (homosexuals and junkies).

It's only now that the majority of those living with HIV-AIDS in the world are heterosexual Africans that some of these condemning voices have quieted down somewhat. But I knew from early on that AIDS wasn't just a gay disease.

Although I wasn't active in the church when I came to

Oakland, I did become involved with the AIDS Project of the East Bay, which was run by an educator named Steve Johnson. What drew me to that project was outreach work I had done while I was at Greater Mount Pleasant back in Memphis.

In Memphis I had worked as a chaplain on the fifth floor of the Regional Medical Center—known as the Med—which was where most of the HIV-AIDS clients stayed. I was appointed to the AIDS ward by the head chaplain there, Wanda Davis. Obviously the role demanded someone open-minded, and because of the life I had lived I was a good choice.

What I saw was both eye-opening and heart-breaking. Seeing people in physical pain that you cannot alleviate is hard, of course, and humbling, but seeing them in such great emotional and spiritual pain was harder still.

There were men and women on that ward, heterosexual, bisexual, and gay, stricken by opportunistic infections, some of whom did recover, at least for a while, some of whom would return again and again, and many who would die. What appalled me was how many of them had been totally deserted in their hour of need—their partners, their families were nowhere to be seen. It made me appreciate all the love and support I had received throughout my life from my families and friends. That, too, was humbling, as realizing how lucky you have been always is.

Seeing these suffering people deserted in that way made me realize I had no right to complain, and it made me value those I love all the more.

It also made me go beyond my duties and become a friend to those lonely and at times despairing men and women—because I do believe that when you've been fortunate you should give something back to society.

I can recall helping with a funeral money-wise.

And burnt onto my mind is the face of a young woman who had lost her child to AIDS shrieking out to God, "Take me and leave her here! It's not her fault!" She, herself was HIV+, but her daughter had died first, over in another hospital. I had had to tell her that her daughter had passed. How can you comfort someone in that situation? But I did the best I could.

One of our duties was to inform the families when a patient passed away. Sometimes the family just didn't want to know. Other times they would come in, and we would take them to the family meeting room and let them express their pain and anger and grief, and offer what support we could.

So many of the people on the ward were filled with self-hatred and guilt over having the disease, I would urge them to disregard the hell-bound sermons that had filled their minds and brought them to that defeated, self-loathing mentality. I approached them with humility and great compassion—after all, with all the sex I'd had, how easily I could have been lying where they were!—and encouraged them to focus on a personal relationship with God. To study the Bible for themselves, pray for guidance and, with God's help, come to their own conclusions about the rightness of their lives and what they could do with what remained of the time allotted them.

And I thought about my life, and how my father left my mother before I was born. How I was expected to die, but God said, "Not so." And then my mother left me, retreating behind the veil of her madness, leaving me alone and utterly helpless. And how I came to find myself in a foster home where there were loving, caring, sharing parents who loved me as their own. They gave me their love unconditionally, and it's because of that that I'm able to love others, not selfishly but as if they're my own. I've learned the value of unconditional love. And, through working at the Med, I learned the value of compassion.

So even before reaching Oakland I had been involved in supporting those living with HIV-AIDS. But until I became involved in the East Bay project I had never learned much about the medical side of the virus. My role had been spiritual, not informational.

Ernest Height was the director of education, and he and Steve Johnson allowed me to come in and learn. I learned not only about the way the disease works and the different medications and their effects, but also about housing needs and housing policies, government policies on health and welfare, and the way organizations are funded and run.

One part of the project Steve was running that I was immediately drawn to was the Brother to Brother network for black gay men, and I became involved on a volunteer basis. We did educational and outreach work in the community and produced a magazine called *Whassup*, which was an educational and informational magazine for black gay men about safe sex, HIV, and AIDS. I was *Whassup*'s first cover model.

At the same time as that I was still hitting the clubs and bars and dancing to earn a living. I had visited Oakland a good few times before I moved there, and had gotten to know the gay scene pretty well.

It was when I was stripping at a club called Cables Reef that I met my next lover, a handsome, masculine, light-skinned man named 'Randy'. He was well-groomed, had the body of a Greek god, and was a hair-stylist. Actually "hair-stylist" doesn't do him justice; he owned and ran two salons, and was wealthy and successful. We began seeing each other and after a little while I moved into his home.

Randy treated me good. All I had to do was be in the house, go shopping whenever I felt like it over at "the City" (which is what people in Oakland call San Francisco), make sure I looked good for him when he came home, and enjoy life. He was always extremely nice to me, and I never wanted-ed for anything.

But inevitably he also wanted constant attention, which was boring to me, and he wanted sex all the time, which I did not, and that got on my nerves.

He was in love with me but with all I had gone through in relationships over the previous ten or more years I just found it impossible to love him in return. At that point in my life I don't think I could have really given my love to any man.

Also, although our apartment was nice—we lived in a middle-class area by the lake—I found Oakland boring, and

I found our life together boring.

I was young and stupid. It was another relationship I messed up, and I look back on it with regret. Not because I failed to love Randy—love isn't a choice—but because I was to go on and develop such a focused and ambitious attitude towards my career in the adult entertainment industry. It would have meshed so well with his shrewd business-mindedness in regards to his own career, and we could have made an amazing team. We could have been a real gay power couple. Instead I was a dizzy stripper with some sort of social conscience who got bored with being a kept boy.

Love IS a choice. It's the duty of all religious believers. We can't be attractive / like everyone & we choose our friends, but our fellow men we must love.

CHAPTER FOURTEEN:

CITY OF ANGELS

Randy had family in Los Angeles, and one time he pressed me to accompany him there on a visit. Being as I was bored sitting around in his apartment in Oakland I agreed to go, but grudgingly.

"When you're visiting your family, just drop me off at the club," I told him. Which shows you what condition our relationship was in by that point. As does the fact that he did as he was told. He dropped me where I wanted to go, and he left.

By "the club" I meant a large black gay club at one end of Crenshaw Boulevard called the Catch One that I knew from occasional previous visits to L. A.

While I was there I met a fine boy named 'Guy', who had a nice muscular booty. He lived round the corner from the club, on Bronson Avenue. We went back to his apartment and I just wore his ass out. Then I came back to the hotel

Randy and I were staying at to shower and change.

As the water streamed down on my head in that hotel bathroom something clicked over in my brain—I realized I wanted to stay in L. A. What did I have back in Oakland? Most of my clothes, and that was about it. Nothing that mattered to me. Nothing I couldn't replace.

Returning to the club I called Guy, and forty minutes later he was there. He had his car, and we drove back to my hotel. I quickly packed my bags and left.

I doubt Randy was surprised when he turned up to find an empty hotel room, no bags, no note, no me.

Because I'm a people person, when I go to a club I don't just look at folks, and I'm not necessarily just there for sex— I talk to people.

Although I was fairly much new to L. A. I quickly built up a social network. One good friend I made early on was a guy named 'Henry'. Originally from Kansas City, he now lives in Atlanta and works as an insurance adjuster, but back then he was more looking to have fun like we all were. He's a real nice guy; he'd give you the shirt off his back, and he was a gift to me as a friend.

Henry was rooming with a straight guy named 'Maurice', who was very gay-friendly but never fucked around with the guys, in a friend's guest house. My good fortune was that they were looking for a third guy to share with them, and Henry invited me to become part of their household. I was pleased to accept.

When I arrived at their building I had a weird sense of having been there before. It took a moment for the penny to drop—the address was 1134, Bronson Avenue, and the apartment block opposite was where Guy lived.

I went on to make two more friends around that time, one considerably older than me, the other somewhat older, 'Irving' and 'Terence'. Irving became a good close friend. He was never afraid to tell me when he thought I had stepped out of line. "Man," he would say, "you need to think about that—that's wrong." Or: "You need to apologize to that person—what you did there was wrong."

By a coincidence Terence was Guy's ex, and since by the time I got to know Terence I had also found out that Guy had somewhat of a reputation for using people, I kept quiet about my little involvement with Guy.

Guy became involved with another guy who became a friend of mine, 'Dwight'. I always suspected that Guy didn't so much like Dwight as what he thought Dwight could do for him. Actually it was me who introduced Guy to Dwight, at a Black Gay Pride event we attended, Splash, in Houston, Texas. Anyway, Irving, Terence, Guy, and me, we were all good friends. Guy was the least trustworthy, the most fair-weather, but we all had fun together.

One year we went across to New York, for that city's first-ever Black Gay Pride. Terence, who by then owned an accounting firm, arranged everything—the flights, the hotel rooms—and we paid our shares. As we were all good friends we shared a huge suite together, had breakfast and went out to dinner together.

We had a really good time, and we all said it would be great to go again the following year, but when the time to

MY LIFE IN PORN

arrange it came around I couldn't reach Terence. I'd call and call and never get a reply. Eventually I found out that he'd taken ill and a very short time later had passed away.

To lose one of my running mates, somebody who was so full of fun and who so enjoyed life, was deeply shocking to me. It was the end of our little group as Guy was never as close-knit as me, Terence, and Irving.

Irving and I remained close, however. Later on, when I moved back to Memphis, he would come and visit for my birthday and we would do things together: travel, take rooms, and go to Atlanta. We were never sexually active with each other, we were just the best of friends.

Just last year I got a call from Irving's brother, and immediately I knew something was wrong because I had never met his brother.

"Irving thinks the world of you," he said. "He loves you to death. He would always talk about you."

I was driving home from the gym. I was like, "What's next?"

"Irving's no longer with us," he said.

"What do you mean?" I asked.

And his brother told me how Irving had been working out at the local YMCA, and he had had a heart attack and passed away right there in the gym, before anyone had even had the chance to call for an ambulance. Gone in the twinkling of an eye.

I lost my old Memphis friend Dee in a similar way in the same year as Irving. I had given a fish fry the Friday of my weekend birthday bash. I rented out a restaurant and Dee came to the fish fry. He was grumbling about not feeling well, but as he looked like a million dollars I didn't pay any attention.

The very next day he was rushed to the hospital. They had to open his heart and use a balloon to open a major artery, and he didn't make it. And so it was that I lost the second friend who I could talk to about anything, who I would consult about all my business decisions, who gave me comfort and support and trust.

It's very difficult to lose dear friends: only time heals, and even then the healing is never complete.

But back then it was me, Maurice, Terence, Irving, and Guy, the five of us out for wild times in the City of Angels, in search of sex, romance, and adventure. We were our own soap opera, our own drama series, our own sitcom.

It was one slow evening at the Catch One that I made my entry into the world of adult movies.

CHAPTER FIFTEEN:

TOTALLY TIGHT

I was at the Catch One one sweaty, Saturday night when this guy came up to me. His name was Dwen Curry, and he was a fashion designer who subsequently went on to design costumes for the cult black gay television series "Noah's Arc." He also appeared in the show as a character named Romeo, a friend of the lead character's who just happens to be a fashion designer. Dwen has a flamboyant style but he's also very street smart and tough-minded—he's had a hard life and he's nobody's fool. We knew each other from being on the club scene.

"Are you bored?" he asked me.

I nodded.

"I can take you to where there are gonna be a whole lot of masculine men fucking like crazy," he said, his manner offhand, as if that was nothing.

"Yeah?" My manner was cool in return.

"Yeah," he said. "Are you about ready to go?"

"Sure," I said. I looked round at the same old faces going through the same old routines. "Whatever." I had been leaning against the bar. I pushed myself off of it. "Why not? Let's go."

We made our way out of the club and to Dwen's car. He drove us to a sex club over on Cahuenga Boulevard in Hollywood called Throb. It was fronted, and not only fronted but also actually owned, by the black gay porn star Paul Hanson. Maybe he's not so well-remembered now, but he was one of the old school, that first generation of performers on video who came up in the mid-Eighties, along with Gene LaMarr, Randy Cochran, T.J. Swann, Joe Simmons, and many others, some of whom are no longer with us, and with some of whom I was to work in my very first movie.

It's hard to remember because things have changed so rapidly, and young folks will have no memory of this at all, but home video was the start of a revolution in porn. Before people had video-recorders in their own homes, if they wanted to see hard-core sex they would have to go to a sex-cinema. That is, they would have to leave their homes, go to a place where they might be recognized, buy a ticket from a stranger to whom they would have to confess exactly the sort of sex they were turned on by through buying that ticket, and if they wanted to jerk off to the film they were watching they would be doing it in semi-public and might get busted by the police and humiliated.

With home video they still had to take the movie to the counter in the video store or adult bookstore to rent it, but everything else about the experience was totally private. And, of course, like today people could buy things by mail-order and so have no personal contact with anyone at all while getting hold of their pornography.

The other big change that was happening was that the quality of video tape was constantly improving. At first it wasn't seen as a viable medium for erotica because, unlike film, it was harsh, emphasized every flaw and blemish, and produced a cheap, ugly effect. Makers of porn films back then, who shot their movies on 16 or 35 millimeter filmstock, didn't see it as having a future. But video was much cheaper than film, it got better, and people started buying VCRs for their homes. VCRs were getting cheaper, and like the internet today, the idea of seeing sexually explicit images in the privacy of your own home was a powerful incentive for owning—or at least renting—one. So technological change created a new market and a new product which, before the early Eighties, didn't exist at all: the porn video.

One spin-off from the cheapness of the new format was the possibility of making money from producing so-called "minority interest" videos. That was when black gay porn videos started to be made, around 1986 I guess, and that led to the first wave of black gay porn stars, of which Paul Hanson was one.

I wasn't a big consumer of porn—mostly I was out there doing it—but I had seen some of Paul's films and I knew who he was, and Dwen introduced us.

Throb was a sex club, a really wild place, and the minute I walked through the door I knew I was in for the best time of my life because it was filled with these military guys, servicemen up from San Diego on furlough, gorgeous, fit, hard-bodied masculine men, and I had so much ass to fuck it was unbelievable. I had no inhibitions, and I just fucked one guy after another—black, white, Latino, I didn't care. It's amazing how many men will let you fuck them if you come on strong enough and you make it known that's what you want to do to them. Maybe it had to do with these guys being in the military—all that pressure towards being manly in a rigid, fixed kind of way—maybe getting fucked by a big black man was some kind of release from that. I don't know. Just a guess. But they sure were happy to let me fuck them.

Evidently Paul had noticed the way I was making all the boys holler, because later on, when Dwen and I were leaving—Paul had closed down the club and we were all on our way out the door—he asked me, "Say, have you ever thought of doing porn?"

Well, I remembered going into the adult bookstores along Summer Avenue back in Memphis when I was a teenager. I remembered seeing the rows of videos on the shelves starring people like Paul, Randy Cochrane, Gene LaMarr, and others, and thinking, "I wouldn't mind trying that some day." And even, "I'd like to give that a try." It wasn't an obsession; just something I'd thought about like most gay men have at some point or other thought about, especially if they enjoy sex and have a big dick and a good physique. But even though I'd just gotten through fucking a whole row of guys in the middle of a sex-club, which was hardly the behavior of a shy guy, it wasn't something I particularly thought I would ever do for real. And now here was Paul Hanson the porn-star, who I'd seen fucking and being fucked on film, asking me had I ever thought of making an adult video.

"No, he hasn't!" Dwen said before I could reply, cutting across me, apparently taking the view that going to a sex club was fine, but doing porn would be that crucial bit too trashy.

"I can speak for myself," I grumbled. But that kind of brought the conversation to an end, and Paul turned away to take care of some business or other back in the club and the moment was past.

"Time to go," Dwen said.

But before we left I wrote my number down on a scrap of paper and slipped it to Paul behind Dwen's back. I didn't really expect Paul to call me. The whole night had had an unreal quality to it, and the next morning it was as if it had all been a dream or a hallucination. However, a week later to the day the phone rang and it was Paul.

"So," he said.

"So," I said.

"Are you serious about wanting to make adult films?" he asked.

"I'm serious," I said.

"Then there are some guys who want to meet you. I told them about you, and they're interested."

"Cool," I said. "When and where?"

Paul arranged for me to meet these producers he knew and had worked with, and take it from there. I had no idea what they would be like. My mind ran the gamut from Mafia types to seedy, exploitative voyeurs, but they turned out to be a pleasant young couple, two nice looking gay white guys, and they ran a video company called Totally Tight that's still in business today. They invited me to their home, a spacious, comfortable house on Laurel Canyon up in the Hollywood hills, and we got to know each other a little and we talked some business.

Because I knew Paul had told the guys about my uninhibited performance at his club I felt I was in a good position to deal. I made sure I walked into that room radiating confidence. I wore well-fitting shorts and a tight gym vest so as to show off my physique to best advantage, but nothing too trashy or provocative; I didn't want to come off like a ho. I made sure to be on time, so that they would know they were dealing with someone professional-minded and considerate of others, and I was polite, practical, and businesslike throughout our meeting. Actually it was easy because the guys were well-mannered and straightforward with me.

At the end of the meeting they asked me if I would like to be in a video and I said yes. They told me it was to be called *Ebony Knights*, and it would be a black gay film. I was to shoot one scene, for which I would be paid $3,500.

The guys offered me a contract to sign exclusively with their company, but I said no to that. Even though I had yet to make a single film I had a premonition that being a porn actor was something that could propel me up into the stratosphere of success. If that happened I didn't want to find myself tied to any one company, or to a contract that might end up failing to pay me what I was worth.

Of course I didn't say any of that to the guys. As I recall I expressed to them that since this was my first film I didn't know if I would enjoy it or want to do any more, and so I didn't want to feel pressurized or under any obligation to do more films for them or anyone else. They said they understood and we agreed upon my fee and terms informally. We ended the meeting with a handshake and a shooting date agreed on for a couple of weeks later. My journey into the world of hardcore gay porn had begun.

Driving back to my apartment on Bronson Street I felt quietly excited and full of anticipation. The sky was blue and huge, the sun was bright, it was all good.

I had only one qualm about being in a porn movie, but it was a big one: I was dating someone.

He was a beautiful Latino boy named 'Renoly'. He was from a well-off family and lived in an upscale apartment complex just off La Brea. Since I was still sharing my apartment on Bronson with a friend it was only natural that I was spending a lot of time over at Renoly's place, and we were slowly growing closer and our feelings for each other were deepening. While we weren't sexually exclusive, I hated the thought that Renoly would see me in a porn video.

My sudden squeamishness may sound a bit ridiculous; after all, hadn't I just been fucking one guy after another at Paul's sex club in front of whoever and enjoying it? I guess the difference is that Renoly didn't know about that, and even if he guessed he didn't know for certain, so he could put it out of his mind and not be hurt by it. But a porn video? Even back then I realized that it would be a hard thing to watch your mate being graphically intimate with someone else, especially on the permanent record and for the entertainment of strangers.

I reached for my cell and hit up Paul Hanson.

"He's gon' see it," I worried to Paul. "For that reason I'm struggling with doing it, you know?"

"Well, it's up to you," Paul said. "It's your call." He knew better than to try and push anyone into doing porn—anything like that, you have to make up your own mind. The consequences are too serious. He was acting like a counselor, just bouncing my thoughts back at me, not directing me this way or that.

"I tell you what," I said eventually. "I'm gon' try it." The minute those words came out my mouth I knew I was making the right decision. "Yeah," I said. "I'm gon' try it. After all," I justified to myself as I hung up the phone, "chances are it's very rare he's gon' see this one."

Which just shows how wrong you can be! I guess it's the private nature of porn, you can imagine most nobody apart from yourself seeing whatever movie or magazine you're looking at. You don't realize hundreds of thousands of copies of each title are being run off some assembly line somewhere and sold to consumers world-wide.

It took me a while to wake up to how vast the adult entertainment industry is, and when I did I was amazed. But I'm getting ahead of myself.

The two weeks went by fast. In the meantime I realized that my relationship with Renoly had peaked, and it began to fade out of its own accord. As it turned out I never did have to tell him about the movie.

The day of the shoot arrived. I had a time and an address, and that was it. I didn't know who I would be performing with, and I hadn't spoken to or met the director. Not exactly a sexy setup. Despite all of that I felt relaxed and confident as I slipped behind the wheel of my leased Mercedes-Benz and turned the key in the ignition. I slipped a CD into the player and Reba McEntire's voice soared melodically as I pulled out: I've always had a fondness for country and western. I sang along with Reba as I turned onto Crenshaw Boulevard.

Being a sex performer is a very particular thing. I'll get into the difference between porn actors and porn stars later, but for now I want to talk about just performing. You need to be uninhibited and naturally exhibitionistic. You need to be able to get turned on in all sorts of un-sexy circumstances. You have to both do what you're doing—fuck someone with passion—and *perform* it, make sure you're acting it out in a way that will come across to the viewer. Lots of people like the idea of appearing in a porn film, but very few are suited to it. Even today, when Viagra is used all the time, you'll often see films where the performers fail to maintain their erections, and seem generally self-conscious and embarrassed. And of course it's embarrassing to watch people who are embarrassed.

Now, when I started making movies Viagra wasn't available. They needed performers who could get a hard-on without chemicals and then throw down a hot performance regardless of the cameramen, technicians, and production people standing around while you fuck. For me, attention gave me energy. It always has. It's my Viagra. I looked good and I knew I looked good. From my years of dancing and stripping I was at ease being naked in front of a crowd. I knew from Paul Hanson's sex party that if the guy I was fucking was hot I would have no problems performing, and that being watched would most likely make me fuck even harder. So I drove to the set the morning we were filming with complete confidence in myself and my abilities. I was intrigued and curious, but not nervous.

We were shooting in a gay bar which was closed in the day-time. It was a no-frills production, with a minimum of set and costumes, and no storyline. With very few exceptions that's the way I preferred my films to be—purely about hard fucking, and not cluttered up with the director's artistic vision or literary conceptions. But of course this was my first film, and I had no say in how it looked or where it was set or who I was to be working with. All I knew was that there would be eight or ten black male performers and that I was hired to perform with one of them.

I was lucky in that Paul Hanson was one of the stars of the film. So I had a friend on the set to introduce me to the rest of the cast and show me the ropes. It was a good way to get started in the industry.

Director William Hunter was very professional. He had a

let's-get-it-done attitude and wasn't unduly controlling of how the sex was performed and just let me get on and do my thing.

I was extremely lucky to be paired with Gene LaMarr for my first scene. He was a handsome, moustachioed, caramel-skinned man with soft jheri-curls, a real industry profession-al who had appeared in dozens of films by then, some of which I had seen. By then in his mid-forties, he still had a flawless physique and a great ass. He was free of attitude, and friendly, and I found him extremely sexually attractive, so I had no trouble performing with him.

They had two cameras on us, which is how porn is usual-ly shot, with two or three cameras at once to get all the angles, and various technicians were going back and forth doing stuff the whole time, but the minute I got with Gene I forgot those people were in the room! The sex was so hot they just fell away from my mind. Gene was awesome, up for everything I wanted to do to him, loving me fucking him, and I fucked him so hard the damn table turned over! I was so into it I shocked myself. I was also very verbal, dogging him out while I fucked him and calling him all kinds of bitches.

Most performers aren't at all verbal, and it turned Gene on and added to the memorability of my first performance on video.

In fact that first scene was so successful that William Hunter asked me to do a second one.

"For another $3,500?" I said.

"Yeah," he said.

"Sure," I replied. "I'll do it." And I amazed him and the rest of the cast by shooting my second scene back-to-back with the first one, with hardly a pause for breath. This guy whose name I forget was standing on a ladder. I was wearing a hard-hat, and he went down on me and then I fucked him. It was less memorable than my scene with Gene had been, but it went fine.

After that I cooled off watching another very successful porn-star of the time, Randy Cochrane, who was in the movie and was by then wearing a peroxided goatee and shaving his head, getting fucked every which way over a bar table by a big-built but slightly out of shape Duke Johnson, another guy who appeared in quite a few movies around that time. And of course I watched my man Paul Hanson throw down, though I forget the name of his partner. After that I collected a check for $7,000. It had been around four hours of work.

"Damn," I thought to myself. "I *like* this job."

I got behind the wheel of my Merc and drove home sweaty and energized with plans whirling around my head. This was the moment I had been waiting for. I had found the perfect collision of pleasure with work. I had found my secular vocation. I had found my career.

CHAPTER SIXTEEN:

BECOMING
BOBBY BLAKE

I had hit the ground running. *Ebony Knights* sold well and all of a sudden contracts were landing wham-wham-wham on my doorstep. I was a hot property. And it was at this point that so much of the way I had been brought up kicked in and worked to my advantage. Unlike so many porn performers I approached making adult videos not as an extension of partying but as a career. I brought my parents' business-mindedness to what I was doing, my foster-mother's belief in hard work and her puritan dislike of the excesses of drugs and alcohol, and focused my mind on my career like a laser focuses light through a diamond.

From the beginning I created a persona who could become a brand: Bobby Blake the Porn Star. "Bobby," after my foster-brother, and "Blake" after a professional football player who I had been seeing. When I went to work I became Bobby Blake, domineering and relentlessly aggressive, always sexual, a somewhat violent and scary guy. Then I went home and became myself again: a man capable of love, surrounded by friends.

Although I saw Bobby Blake as a persona distinct from the real me, it took a couple of movies for the Bobby Blake most of my fans know to really crystallize. As a rule I didn't—and don't—watch my own films. I don't even own copies of all my films. But I did watch my first few films to see how I came across, and how I could make my perform-ance more definite and distinctive.

For instance, if you watch *Ebony Knights* it's noticeable that, although I fuck Gene LaMarr real hard, I'm also quite affectionate towards him, kissing, rimming, and even going down on him. That was because there was far more of the real me present in that performance than there would be in the fifty-plus films that followed: I hadn't yet fully split myself off from my porn persona.

As the three years I was making porn films went by Bobby Blake became more aggressive and more violent. The end-term of my persona was my most extreme and final film, which was called *Niggas' Revenge*, and which I'll talk about in greater depth in a later chapter. After that, and at the top of my game, I retired from making adult movies. I'd always tried to progress my persona by making each film I did somehow more daring and extreme than the one before. With *Niggas' Revenge* I'd taken Bobby Blake as far as he could go, and it was time to quit and do something else with my life.

As well as a brand I wanted to build, I had a philosophy

behind Bobby Blake. It evolved out of traveling and going to Pride events throughout the country, both before and after I started to become well-known. I would talk to people and listen to people talking. And sometimes they would dare each other to do things sexually. Or they would say that nobody would ever dare to such-and-such a thing in a film. I would hear that and keep in mind anything they said. And if I could, I would take what they had dared but didn't think that anyone would actually do, and do it. I would bring it to reality, and it would come forth on the screen and cause anyone watching to say, "Wow! I can't believe he just did that!"

I had a plan for Bobby Blake, a burning desire to succeed, and even more than those two things, a determin-ation to be respected at every turn as I did so.

I was also realistic.

Over the years many people have asked me how to go about getting into the adult industry: young guys are forever coming up to me and asking, "Bobby, how can I get into the porn industry? How can I be like you?" And I can tell by the way they express themselves that they're not realistic about what being a porn actor actually involves. Performing in adult films isn't just an extension of having a good time: it's a job, and you need to approach it as one.

Being filmed having sex for a living can take a spiritual and psychological toll on a person. It requires an inner resilience. Many people in the adult industry struggle with alcohol and drug abuse issues because they lack that strength, that toughness of ego. They are often vulnerable, unstable people who lack focus and need attention, and in going into porn they're seeking it in a dangerous way. It wasn't a need for attention that led to me performing in adult films, but a desire for attention motivates a lot of people, and being a porn actor is rarely a healthy way of getting it. I have always had all the attention I wanted, and I was entirely used to being an object of desire because of my many years working as an exotic dancer and a stripper. So I was ready to perform in front of an audience un-inhibitedly and un-self-consciously. I could allow the people around me to add to my energy even if they were just a bored-looking camera crew and technicians. Many people—most people—can't do that.

Also, would-be performers often confuse being a porn *actor* with being a porn *star*. In fact, porn films are just like Hollywood films in this respect: most actors are not stars, and never will be. Stars can get star treatments; actors don't get star treatment. Stars are in demand and command good money. Actors are often short of work and often don't get well-paid when they do work.

I became a star. I'm known all over the world, and my work in adult films has brought me respect, money, and the adoration of tens, maybe hundreds of thousands of people. I've bought luxury cars, I've hung out with film stars and sports stars from the mainstream. I've been in their homes and I've lived the high life and enjoyed it. I had the strength of will to control my career and the way I was treated by other people.

I never got an agent. I represented my own self. I'd always felt that if I marketed myself right, if I came across powerfully enough, then I would be in great demand, and that turned out to be true. I handled my own business, and even if I wasn't always popular, I was always respected by whomever I was dealing with. I was successful. But I never let anyone who asks me about getting into the porn business forget that the odds were against me, and that as well as being smart and hard-working, I was also extremely lucky.

I would guess that only about one in one hundred thousand who are involved in the porn industry actually becomes any kind of star, if that many. The rest get used, often abused, and are then dumped and left to rebuild the rubble of their lives.

From the point of view of the porn industry there are always thousands more where *they* came from.

I often use my ex-lover, Flex-Deon Blake, as an example of how ruthless the world of adult entertainment is. I gave him my last name to promote him as a performer. We made films together. He had a beautiful body, great looks, and ambition, but he never reached the level I reached. He never got to the top. Being involved in porn just magnified the problems he had; it didn't solve them.

Rather than getting involved in porn I always counsel young people to get an education instead, and equip themselves with the tools they're going to need to be successful in society. Gain knowledge that no one can take from you. Educate yourself so you can have the best life this world has to offer. Set your sights on being a lawyer or a doctor. Don't spend your whole life in a nightclub or in gay bars. Don't make the gay world your whole world. You can be yourself but live in the wider world, too. Young gay people don't need to be told that they can't be part of the world of education and conventional achievement. They don't need to be told that becoming part of the gay adult entertainment industry is the best way to express themselves, tempting as it is. There's a whole world out there beyond that: don't turn your back on it.

In any case, if they must go into the adult entertainment industry then they need the intelligence and education to deal with the negative as well as the positive aspects of it. They need the education to be able to make the adjustments to step back into what I call mature society, because for sure you can't be a porn actor forever.

Now, you may be thinking I'm telling people to do what I say, not what I've done. But one thing it's important to notice is that the adult industry has changed since I was performing seven, eight, nine years ago. It doesn't pay like it used to pay. Nowadays a lot of companies get these guys off the street, many of 'em desperate for an early payday, clean 'em up, use them for a shoot, give them a hundred dollars and throw them back. Or you have internet-based setups like Cocoboyz and Cocodorm, featuring very young performers who the company has no interest in promoting or building up into stars or even names: they're just an interchangeable parade of cute, pliable youngsters in need of a quick buck who think that spending a couple of weeks on display in the 'dorm' will be an easy way of making some money, all the while getting drawn into unsafe sex practices by an unscrupulous management.

Again, changes in medical treatments have changed the

face of gay adult films. When I started appearing in them safe sex practices were always carefully observed because HIV-AIDS was seen as a death sentence. Cum was never ingested, and condoms were always worn for fucking. Now, to an extent that's troubling, young people, particularly young black gay men, are becoming infected at an extremely high rate because they see the new anti-retrovirals as magic bullets. They blot out of their minds the side-effects—liver damage, lypodistrophy, and so on—and the likelihood of eventual treatment failure and premature death. Now there is a pressure on new young performers to have unsafe sex. "Barebacking" is talked about as daring, outlaw, taboo, and therefore exciting, and young guys are offered extra money if they'll do it.

I made adult movies over a period of around three years. During that time I made around fifty films, but if you check my filmography online you'll find a lot more titles listed. That's down to the fact that a lot of the films that have come out with my name on them since I retired are made up out of bits of old films I'd already done, edited together and given a new title. In porn as a performer you get a flat fee for your performance, so I don't make a cent out of these stitched-together DVDs. But I'm not resentful: I got paid at the time, and I got paid well, and they help keep me in the public eye and allow new viewers to sample the Bobby Blake experience today.

CHAPTER SEVENTEEN:

THE JOB

Even today when they meet me people are surprised that I'm friendly, open, and intelligent rather than boorish, ignorant, and aggressive to the point of violence. I have to explain to them that Bobby Blake was a character, a persona I would snap into for work purposes. I would go on-set and for me it was a change of character so extreme it was almost like changing my sex—I was like Linda Carter whirling around and turning into Wonder Woman, or Clark Kent going into a phone booth and coming out as Superman. At home I was me. On set I was Bobby Blake, and Bobby was there to work. To fuck. So I would turn up and perform—I would go into a mental zone where I enjoyed fucking these other guys as hard as I could, humiliating and using them and calling them all kinds of bitches.

To me the sex aspect of shooting porn was always easy. You would have two or three cameras on you. You would only actually fuck for twenty, maybe thirty minutes, and the footage could be edited together to run for over an hour. I never had trouble performing, so to me it was an amazingly easy way to make money, and that's why I made so many films in such a comparatively short period.

I was a sex professional. But if I was professional then I demanded that everyone else be professional in return, and that made me unpopular with some people in the industry, because I always demanded I be treated with respect and had zero tolerance for bullshit.

For instance: one time I was doing a gang-bang movie. I don't know if it ever got released, but I suppose it probably did, or the footage we shot turned up in some movie or another. I had quickly gotten to the point where I didn't keep track of the product. We were shooting in a huge house in Hollywood that was the size of a damn palace. The icebox was as big as a bedroom, there was an elevator you took from floor to floor, and Madonna's house was just down the road. It was an awesome place, a mansion, and the producers had gotten the owner to lend it to them for one day to make this film.

They had brought a guy over from Atlanta to be gang-banged, a white boy. He had taken something to deaden his ass so he could take all that dick, but pretty soon after we had started in he got a tear and started to bleed. Apart from the issue of harming someone, any sign of blood was of course a big safe-sex problem, and so the shoot had to be stopped.

We were all standing around, me and the other actors, wondering what was going to happen. The crew was packing up the cameras and lights. The producers noticed us waiting around. "Y'all can go home now," they said, just like that.

MY LIFE IN PORN

The cast—eight or nine black guys—looked at each other but didn't say anything. After a long moment I stepped up.

"We gon' get paid?" I asked.

"We can't pay you today," one of the producers said. "The movie didn't get made."

"So what?" I said, getting mad. I mean, here I was, I had turned up ready to work. It wasn't my fault the guy I was supposed to fuck was bleeding in the ass. "We goin' home with our Goddamn checks!" I said angrily.

"No way."

"We don't get paid today, ain't no motherfucker leaving this house," I said. "And I know the owners want you out of here by tonight."

It was a Mexican standoff: I wasn't going nowhere. Paul Hanson, who was in the movie with me, was touching my arm and saying, "Bobby, c'mon, they'll send us the checks. Let's go."

"No," I told him. "We gon' get paid *now*." I turned back to the producers with determination written all over my face. "You guys better start writing out those checks and they better be good."

And they did.

And they were.

So I became spokesmodel on that set, and it wouldn't be the last time I would take on that role. See, there was at that time in the porn industry, as in many other areas of business, the assumption that you could treat black and other non-white people worse than white people. Even veterans like Paul Hanson were used to accepting crummy conditions and poor treatment. But from the beginning I was determined not to give in to that kind of racism. I had a different mindset: I demanded respect, and I do believe that in being demanding I raised the bar for how non-white minorities could be treated in gay porn.

A sillier version of the same thing came up when we were shooting another gang-bang movie. This was called *Black Raven Gang Bang* and it had the same setup as a lot of my interracial movies: a bunch of black dudes mostly fucking some white boy. Actually a lot of those movies set themselves up that way, but then when it came to shooting them the African-American performers would often end up fucking each other as well as the white boy just to make sure plenty of sex was happening at all times, so they weren't as one-note as they looked on the box covers. This was true of this movie, where the whole film was mostly one big group scene with just a few cutaways.

Black Raven Gang Bang was produced by a company called XTC who later got shut down owing to a whole lot of tax problems, I believe, and it was shot on the cheap in a bar. Now at this bar they had this four hundred-pound guy who worked there called Spanky. And at one point while we were shooting it had gotten real hot and he took off his shirt, and at the sight of his fat ass half-naked it was like death had come upon the models. Dicks drooped and sex-drives stalled. The whole rhythm of the orgy completely collapsed. I kind of feel bad saying it, but that's how it was.

By then it was late. Everyone was tired and the situation was frustrating. Once again I stepped up as spokesmodel. I insisted the shoot be stopped for the day and made the producers get us all hotel rooms and order us food so we would be in good shape to regroup the following day. I even got us another day's pay. I had already come once, and my attitude was, if you want me to come twice in a movie, you have to pay me twice.

I never had any trouble putting myself forward for a leadership role. I had done it in the church, back in Greater Mount Pleasant, and I saw no reason not to do the same thing in the world of adult entertainment.

From the first I knew what was needed to make a porn movie work. Sometimes my idea of what was needed was at odds with what a producer or director wanted, but I always stood up for what I thought was right. For instance, I made a film with Paul Barresi called *The Underboss*, in which I played a boxer named Mighty Joe who gets involved with the Mafia. Paul's an interesting character in his own right, a heterosexual, married porn actor who also wrote, directed, and produced adult films, and I went on to make two further films with him: a prison-break movie called *The Iron Cage*, and my favorite of the three, a Civil-War-set period piece titled *Black Brigade*.

As well as writing and directing the film, Paul also appeared in it as the Underboss himself, a non-sexual role. Heterosexual porn star Ron Jeremy appeared in the film, too, similarly in a non-sexual role. It was an expensive, upscale production.

Anyway, we had shot the movie and there we were doing

the photo shoot for the box-cover of *The Underboss* and Paul was getting on my nerves. He was being bitchy and controlling and a perfectionist, and it was wearing me down. Usually doing a box-cover takes about thirty minutes; we were still standing under the glare of the lights five *hours* later as he pressed the photographer to deliver that perfect shot. Paul's intention was to create a cover that would look like a big-budget mainstream movie poster, like *The Godfather* or something.

Now I'm the type of person who understands that box-covers don't sell movies. Good hard fucking sells movies. Especially when it comes to black movies. Black movies are different than their white counterparts: white movies are more likely to have stories while black movies are more hardcore, more direct. Paul liked to have plots, and that was fine: *Black Brigade* was a real nice movie, and wearing the Civil War uniforms both made an interesting and even touching historical point, and looked sexy and different. But I really had no tolerance for an excessive amount of unnecessary clutter getting tacked onto our core business: fucking.

I didn't even wear makeup for a box-cover shoot. One, it wasn't my style: my image wasn't being pretty like, say, Tyson Cane with his soft looks, (of whom more later). And two, that way when fans meet me they're never disappointed in my appearance because I haven't used a mess of foundation to cover over blemishes, spots and bags under my eyes.

So there Paul was prolonging and prolonging the shoot, and we must have taken hundreds of photos and still we were standing there. Finally I ran out of patience. I walked off the set, picked up a garden hoe that was leaning against a wall, and banged it on the ground.

"Look, Paul," I said, "write me my Goddamn check because I'm done here." The photographer had his camera pointed my way. "Nobody better shoot another damn roll," I said, eyeballing him.

The photographer—I forget his name, but he was a nice guy—looked over at Paul. "Paul," he said, "do you want me to carry on shooting?"

"If you shoot I'll whack the hell out of you!" I told him. He quickly lowered his camera. "You want your check too?" I asked him. "Cause if you want it he gon' write your damn check, too. Right now. 'Cause we're gon' go."

Paul got real mad. He wrote my check and his hand was trembling with rage as he signed it off. "My uncle, he's in the Mafia," he blustered. "He's gon' make you pay for this—big time!"

"Well, *he* might, but if *you* try and do it you'll damn well walk home," I said. "You don't scare me with that bullshit."

And I left. And I'm still here. And I'm sure Paul Barresi has no love for me, and no doubt he thought I was arrogant because of the way I took control of the situation, but by then my star power was strong enough that he worked with me twice more anyway, on *Black Brigade* and *Iron Cage*.

Star power meant that after only four or five movies I could choose who I worked with. It meant I could command higher fees. And my reputation for assertiveness no doubt headed off a whole lot of bullshit at the pass. No one ever wrote me a bad check, and I always got paid. And if some people didn't like me, so what? I was in show-business, not show-friends.

In fact, I got on well with most of the directors I worked with. I even got on well with Paul most of the time, although he would almost always try and do something to fuck with me. Like in *Iron Cage* he made the guy I was supposed to be fucking dress in drag. He was a gorgeous white guy, but there was no way I was going to fuck him while he was dressed as a woman. Hell, no. So we had a fight over that. I won that fight too, but I always suspect Paul had set it up deliberately to see if he could get me to do something I didn't want to.

Not only directors: I got on well with the crews as well— the camera and technical people. They were mostly white guys and probably most of them were straight, but they were good people, very much all about business. Sometimes I would hear one of them say to another, "Damn, he fucked that boy *down*!" and they would go around the industry talking about how I used the bottom guys, adding to my reputation as a premier top-man.

The first interracial movie I did was directed by Chi Chi LaRue, the drag queen. She's probably the most famous porn director in the world. She's an individualist and a perfectionist, very professional, very good at what she does. The movie was produced by All Worlds and was called *In The Mix*. In it a group of preppy white boys venture into a black bar where Bam, Kevin Kemp, Tyson Cane, Richard Reyes and myself are sitting around in black leather. At first the white boys want to leave, but they end up staying and a series of hot scenarios follow, climaxing with an interracial orgy. It was an odd experience in that there were actually people—regular patrons—in the bar while we were filming our scenes. Chi Chi had to get them to sign waivers in case they accidentally appeared in any of the shots.

Although having an audience is fine by me it did get to some of the other models, because watching us fuck made the customers want some dick as well, and they would damn near follow you wherever you went in the hope of getting some action. But in the end it was a well-made film that looked good. Chi Chi respected me, and I respected her, and I had fun.

It was on the set of *In The Mix* that I first met Tyson Cane. He's a very pretty black fellow-performer who was presented as gay porn's answer to Tyson Beckford, hence his name. We weren't in any scenes together except the climactic orgy scene, which was a relief to me because Tyson Cane was the bitch from hell. He was always in need of something, always wanting more makeup and generally demanding attention and slowing things up. But if he was the bitch from hell, then I was the dad from hell: I kept him in line. I felt like he was kissing the producer's ass to get on while being unduly demanding towards the performers he was working with. I got on his ass about being professional in what he was doing, and I guess he eventually took my words to heart, because he now produces and directs his own movies and is doing good. He teamed up with a Latino guy named Enrico Vega, their company's called Cane-Vega productions and they do racially diverse movies.

I went on to do quite a few other interracial films such as *Zebra Love* with the director Pete Goesinya, but mostly I did all-black/blatino films. I worked with pretty much every director there was, and for pretty much every company there was, including Catalina, which was probably the most prestigious of them all, and at that time to be a black man starring in a lead role in a Catalina film was somewhat groundbreaking. I not only made gay films, I appeared in a number of bisexual ones as well, of which my favorite would be *Goldilocks and the Three Bi-Bears*. *Goldilocks and the Three Bi-Bears* also starred my first porn partner, Gene LaMarr, which was part of what made it so enjoyable to work on.

I never did straight porn because as a man there was no money in it—all the star power went to the females, and the male performers were often sad cases happy to appear in a movie for next to nothing because it meant they got to fuck a hot girl for once. The only advantage to appearing in straight porn would be that as a man you don't have to look so good. Look at probably the most famous straight male porn star of them all, Ron Jeremy. Whereas in gay porn the viewers are very particular and you have to work hard to maintain a high-grade look to satisfy them.

I worked with Pacific Sun, Jet Set, US Male, Dreamland, Filmco, Pleasure Productions, All Worlds, and In-X-Cess. But the company I worked with most often was Bacchus, and the director I worked with most often was Edward James.

CHAPTER EIGHTEEN:

MY PORN
MENTOR

One of my greatest pieces of good fortune during the time I
was involved in the adult entertainment industry was that
early on in my film-making career I met one of the gay porn
world's most successful and prolific directors and producers,
Edward James. I was introduced to him by Paul Hanson and
from the first we connected. We were very different people—
he was a young white guy, straight, married, with a beautiful
wife and kid—but he became a best friend and a mentor to
me. He showed me the ropes. He guided my career and
allowed me to work side-by-side with him. He took me to
business meetings where he was doing contract deals; to parties where I could meet people of influence within the industry. He took me to so many different places he didn't have to.
He was ambitious and totally professional, yet he was also a
humble man, and he was extremely helpful to me for no
other reason than that he saw I was intelligent and focused

enough to be able to be helped in that way.

He would always tell me to take care of my business. "Dot every 'i' and cross every 't,'" he would say, "and someday you'll be at the top. You'll be in control, and they'll have to come to you." And I did. And he was right. And a lot of production companies have come and gone since he gave me that very simple advice, but he's still prospering. He's still smart. He was one of the first porn producer-directors to diversify and use the internet, and his website, Monsterbig.com, is still running today, a decade later.

He sat me down and said, "Bobby, one day you will be king." And then he told me what he meant by that, and it's still a conversation I can remember vividly all these years later.

Edward James' route into gay porn was a peculiar one, but then it's not a career you study for in college. He started out as a model, something he'd been doing since he was a kid. It's a tough business, being a model, and you're always chasing work. Anyway, there he was one day in San Francisco, networking and having lunch with a photographer he knew named Rick Lopez and a bunch of other guys Lopez was working with on a big video shoot that afternoon. He would have been around twenty-one at the time. No one had said what sort of shoot it was, and Edward James hadn't asked. During the meal one of the cameramen got sick, practically passed out from something—flu, food poisoning, something like that. He got so sick he couldn't work. Panic all around: he was the only guy who knew how to use the camera they'd hired.

And then, for no good reason except that you should never turn down work or new experiences, Edward James blurted out, "I can shoot camera!" He was from a comfortable background and as a kid he'd picked up how to work a video camera and shot some little mini-videos for his own entertainment. "I can do it!" he said. "So what are we shooting?"

They told him, "Gay porn."

He thought, "Wow, I'm not so sure about that." But he was a struggling model who needed the money, so he said, "I'm there!" as if it was nothing to him. He shot two scenes, getting paid $350 instead of $500 because he was a novice, had a tough time of it but was liked on the set, and that was how his career as a director of gay porn began.

At that fateful table was another porn director, John Summers. A couple of years later, he and Edward James were both working for a company that produced not only straight but also gay videos called the Planet Group. At that time they were shooting all-white movies, these directors. The received wisdom was that black men were difficult to work with, and these other directors didn't want to be bothered with them. Edward's attitude was that he knew a lot of black people from living in Detroit, he had black friends and he liked black guys. So he thought, Shit, he'd be the one to do it.

Now he says he'd rather shoot black guys than white guys any day; that white guys are too prima donna-ish for him, and he's made dozens and dozens of films with black casts, so he should know. But anyway, that's how come he and I came to meet and become good friends.

Another thing about Edward James, the stand-out thing really, is that he treats his performers real well. He genuinely cares about them. He not only looked out for me, I watched him take guys who'd gotten on drugs and get them into treatment programs. Some of them didn't have a place to live and he would put them in an apartment. Some of them got themselves locked up in jail and he would get 'em out—pay their bail or find them a lawyer. He was concerned for the overall well-being of these guys when a lot of companies just wanted to use them for the hour and throw them back into the streets.

I liked Edward James so I was watching out for him, and I'd get frustrated with him. Christian as I am, I'd ask him, "You know what, why are you dealing with that person? Why do you keep getting that person out of jail? Why do you keep helping them when they don't want to help themselves? Fuck them. Let them suffer. Let them die."

But he would help them anyway.

Today if people ask me about getting into the porn industry, if they're serious about it and can't be dissuaded, it's Edward James I direct them to. Because he's that rare thing, a businessman who's honest and sincere. An employer who cares about his employees.

But if you do want to get into the porn industry, never forget that it can be very wild. It draws a lot of damaged people. There's a lot of drug-abuse. There are links to organized crime. You can get caught up in dangerous situations and criminal complications completely by accident.

For instance: there was a porn actor called Buckhorse Jackson. I appeared with him in the prison break-out movie *Iron Cage*, which Paul Barresi directed after *The Underboss*. He had a huge dick, bigger even than my two well-hung arch-rivals Bam and Kevin Kemp's put together. But I never saw him as a rival to any of us because he was just so painfully dumb.

So Buckhorse had done this movie, and through the industry had met Edward James, who gave Buckhorse one of his business cards, thinking nothing of it.

A week later Edward gets a call from the police: "Do you know a mister so-and-so Jackson?"

"I don't think so," he says. Then he flashes on the surname and says actually yes, he does know him.

"What's your connection with Mister Jackson?" the policeman asks him.

"I don't have a connection with him."

"So how come we found your business card in his wallet?"

"Well," Edward James says guardedly, "I'm a film-maker and I was thinking of casting him in a production. Why? What's going on?"

"He's dead."

It turns out Buckhorse did a bad drug deal and somebody got mad and shot him in the head and killed him.

So that's one way you can get drawn into a bad situation—through business. The other way is the obvious one—through love.

I was briefly involved with a beautiful white bodybuilder named Michael Leigh. He appeared with me in the film *Bam* in 1998. I fucked him twice in that movie, once on my own, and once with Bam standing around watching. But before we appeared in that film together we were seeing each other.

How we met was, I was walking down the street in West Hollywood and all of a sudden this big-ass white body-builder comes up behind me, puts his arms around me, picks me up off my damn feet and says, "Wow! Bobby Blake!"

He was about three times my size. I said, "You big moth-erfucker, you better put me down!"

"Man, I am in love with you," he says, not putting me down. "My wife even knows I have pictures of you all over my wall!"

"Your wife?"

"Yeah."

He puts me down and I turn round and look at him. And I'm looking at this dude, the most gorgeous, gorgeous man I have ever seen, with ass and body and looks for *days*. He wanted to date me and he wanted to do a film with me. In due course I said yes to both, which is how come he wound up appearing in *Bam*.

If you watch *Bam* carefully you'll notice I was very affec-tionate with Michael in that film, more affectionate than I had been with any other performer up to that point, and cer-tainly more affectionate than I was with any performer I had sex with on camera after that. Of course the reason was I had gotten to know Michael before we shot the movie, and we were still sort of dating at the time we filmed.

But like so many porn actors Michael was a mess. He had done time in jail before we met, he was jealous, possessive, and volatile to the point of violence, and our relationship quickly fizzled out after we performed together.

We lost touch after making *Bam*. A couple of years later, when I was a columnist for the magazine *Black Inches,* he wrote me a letter from jail, which was a sad situation. I hope he's gotten his life together since then, but can only feel relieved that I ended our relationship when I did.

I just don't have the patience to deal with that kind of self-destructive mentality. It's one big reason why I've never seriously considered producing or directing my own films. Watching Edward James dealing with all these fucked-up people I realized it wasn't something I had any interest in doing. I'm very professional and business-minded about presenting myself, promoting my interests and making sure I get paid, but I don't really enjoy that kind of managerial work. I know what my strengths are, and I play to them. As Bobby Blake the Porn Star I found I could exert all the control I needed to over my environment without needing to step behind the camera.

So that was one thing that was emphasized to me by my involvement with Michael—that I wouldn't have the patience to direct or produce films. But my scenes with him in *Bam* had another repercussion as well, one that took me totally by surprise.

Maybe reading this book you might be thinking when I talk about how many fans I have, or how obsessed people can become with me, that I'm exaggerating. Maybe you think, "Hey, it's only porn. You jerk off to it and forget it. Who cares?"

To start off with that's pretty much what I thought, too, because most porn is entirely forgettable. But then *Bam* came out. It was a very successful movie and sold widely and well. That year, my second in the adult entertainment industry, I was traveling about a great deal, being sociable and doing appearances at various Black Gay Pride events throughout the South, promoting myself and my films, and I started getting a backlash from the African-American community over my scenes with Michael.

"You nigger-fuck the black ones," a surprising number of people accused me. "And you make love to the white ones."

Now it's true that at the end of the film I do give J. C. Carter, who is an African-American performer, a particularly hard and almost brutal ass-pounding, but the accusation was unjust and somewhat hurtful.

"That particular white guy was someone I was dating," I explained on a number of different occasions. "If you watch my other movies I nigger-fuck the white guys too. But this happened to be somebody I had some feelings towards, which makes a difference."

My explanation was grudgingly accepted. But from then on I knew that my every step was being watched, and that those people watching that film were seriously invested in how I carried myself as a black man. It mattered a great deal to them that I loved my own no less than I loved men of other races, and that that came across on-screen. It was important to them that nothing I did alienated them. Even though I was someone fucking for money I had also on some level to uplift the race.

Absolute craziness that people live such such empty lives that the interested in the actions of a porn star

It was a challenge I rose to.

One example of that would be the credit-sequence idea I came up with for the follow-up film we did after *Bam,* which was titled *Blackballers 2.* It was an Edward James movie for Pacific Sun. In *Blackballers 2* Bam, my then-partner Flex-Deon, and myself are a black street gang in rivalry with a white street gang who we proceed to home-invade, kidnap, and eventually bitch-slap and fuck into submission. It's a hot movie, and I came up with a powerful opening for it that featured the three of us looking masculine as hell, all in para-military black. I was thugged-out in a Kevlar-type padded vest, and we were filmed walking *Shaft*-style down a rough street in downtown L. A. next to a broken-down basketball court, handing out money to the homeless. We gave quite a bit of money away that day, more than you see on film. You can see the homeless people are surprised, grateful, and somewhat confused as to who in hell we are! But that was real money we were handing out, and they were real people in need, so it felt good to be doing something for them, how-ever small.

And you can believe the white guys in *that* movie got nigger-fucked for sure.

CHAPTER NINETEEN:

A BILLION, THRILLION DOLLAR INDUSTRY

The feedback from *Bam* was one signal to me that I was becoming well-known. Another sure sign was going back to Memphis to visit and having friends say to me things like, "Man, I was over at this boy's house. He put this tape in the player" (the films were still mostly on VHS tapes in those days) "and I was fucking him and I looked up and I saw you up there on the TV screen and I said to the guy I was fucking, "Hey, I know that guy!""

And other friends were seeing me on box-covers on shelves in the adult bookstores on Summer Avenue and laughing and saying, "Hell, no, he didn't!"

That was the local news. But my fame was spreading far wider than I had ever imagined it would. How widely my image was becoming known only came home to me when

Bacchus, the company I did the majority of my movies for, and who had always treated me good, booked me to do an autograph signing at the Adult Video News Convention in Las Vegas in January, 1997. This was after I had been making films for somewhat over a year, and I was there as their top model. It was then that I realized how massive the adult entertainment industry is: literally a billion, thrillion dollar industry.

The Adult Video News Convention was part of the larger International Consumer Electronics Show. Adult Video News is the trade journal of the adult film business, reviewing every porn movie that comes out. The industry produces over ten thousand titles a year, and has a turnover of well over four billion dollars annually. And there I was, nappy-headed little me, all grown up and part of that industry.

As well as the numerous trade stalls being run by distribution and production companies a lot of porn stars get brought along to the AVN Convention to add glamour, move product, and meet the fans. It was interesting to me to meet some of the straight stars, guys like Sean Michaels, a well-known and highly successful straight black porn star who not only performs in but also directs his own movies, and runs a production company to distribute them. Sean was there with his wife. He knew my work—a lot of the straight people there did—and he interested me greatly. He was totally different from the person you see on-screen, as I am. He was also totally professional: he's all about business, making money, and has managed to build an empire for himself. I observed him closely and I learned a lot from him, and I commend him for his focus and industry.

Like with any celebrity autograph-signing session we stars would sit at booths all day long over the entire weekend scribbling our signatures on box-covers and photo layouts of ourselves for the lines of fans, smile nicely, and allow ourselves to be photographed with them. What amazed me was how long a line of guys was waiting to see me: hundreds and hundreds of them on any given day. What amazed me even more was how *far* some of them had come to see me. Not only were there guys in that line from every state, there were people from all over the *world*. And not only Europe but Saudi Arabia, Israel, Egypt, and South Africa, places it had never occurred to me that my films would ever reach. I was like, "Wow! I have a worldwide fan base!"

It was then, too, that I first began to experience the obsessive, possessive desire people can develop to have you as a *B* trophy. I could have had a multi-million dollar lifestyle if I had accepted the invitation of a big oil minister to go and live with him in his palace in Saudi Arabia. I *did* take up an invitation to go and stay with a black South African millionaire but that was more like a holiday: just about a week, and then I came straight back home again because I've never been any good at pretending. Your money may be good, but you've got to have more about you than that if you want to be with me. I couldn't have played these guys along, not just to have a lavish lifestyle until they got bored with me and moved on to their next obsession. Now, a lot of other headliners would have done so happily. They're the sort of people who are happy to pretend, and take your money and don't

[handwritten annotation: Rubbish: already admits to that the Persona in porn y not the real him. This is pretend.]

give a damn about it. But me, I just can't pretend.

Probably the craziest and most surprising thing that happened at the AVN Conference was between me and this gorgeous young lady who was sitting in the booth alongside mine. Her name was Krystal and she was doing an autograph signing, too. She was an internet model, not a porn star, but guys were lined up to see her just like they were lined up to see me. She was a stunning blonde, and all these men were offering her money to sleep with them, and of course she was turning them down.

Now, she knew I'd been doing gay movies, but towards the end of the last day she leaned over to me and she whispered, "I want you to fuck me."

"Huh?" I said.

"I want you to fuck me," she repeated, her lips hot against my ear.

I looked over at all those hundreds of guys standing in line, dozens of them so crazy over the idea of being with her they'd pay big bucks for the privilege, and I laughed.

"I don't need to pay for no pussy," I told her as I scrawled my signature across a full-color close-up of my erect dick for an excited, flush-faced fan from Minnesota.

"I'm not expecting you to pay," she said.

Me and my producer closed up the booth around six-thirty or seven that evening, and Krystal rode with us back to our hotel. I invited her up to my room. Well, I must have fucked that woman for a good five hours. I nut' about ten times inside of her. I came so much she probably had my child: she's probably looking for me right now for child support!

And later I thought, "If we'd filmed it we could have sold it, to her fans and mine."

The AVN Conference was a lifetime experience for me. It showed me the vastness of the adult entertainment industry, and it was an eye-opener to me as to how far the Bobby Blake concept had reached out. Over that weekend I must have signed about three thousand autographs.

Before moving on, once again I have to say that times have changed considerably since those days. Back then all the companies operated under the umbrella of AVN. Now there are a lot of little companies where they just pick guys up at the bus stop, clean 'em up a little, shoot the fucking with a regular camera, and sell the results online. The bigger companies are still there, but an increasing share of the market is being taken up by these much smaller, low-budget outfits that have no interest in promoting their performers. So there's much less sense of there being an "industry standard" than there was when I was making films. The results are lower quality, and there's less investment in building up the artists generally.

My next big porn-related event, the Probe Men in Video Awards, was a very different experience, and a much more negative one, because it brought me face-to-face with the racism that pervaded, and to a considerable extent, still pervades the adult film industry.

CHAPTER TWENTY:

NAKED
RACISM

The Probe Men in Video Awards is usually known as the Probies, after the Hollywood club The Probe in which the awards used to be held. It's a yearly people's choice award ceremony for achievement in gay adult films. Fans log on to websites and cast votes for their favorite performers in twenty or so categories. These categories change from year to year, and range from cute ones like "Sexiest Eyes" to more hard-core ones like "Stud You'd Most Like to Spread 'Em For." There are pre-show parties and post-show parties and you can believe there's a lot of wildness going on at those events.

I attended the Probies the same year I was at the Adult Video News Conference. Being Bacchus' top model I had been nominated for Best Newcomer, and I knew it would be an interesting experience and an opportunity to meet people and be seen.

As they do every year, at the start of the ceremony they

projected pictures of various porn stars who had died in the previous twelve months, and one or other of the hosts would say something about each person who had passed, honoring them. That was the year that Joe Simmons died, and so naturally I was expecting them to honor him, but the commemorative section ended without his name even being mentioned.

Well, that riled me, because Joe Simmons was a genuine star. As well as making dozens of black gay movies he had done films with Christopher Rage, who was a white gay director whose work was at the crossroads of shock porn and avant-garde filmmaking, and, under his real name, which was Thomas Williams, Joe had also been a model for the still-notorious photographer Robert Mapplethorpe, appearing in his *Black Book* collection. Mapplethorpe, like Joe, was later to die of AIDS-related complications. Joe also acted in a number of off-Broadway shows in New York. He had gone from being a sexual outlaw—which is how come he met Rage and Mapplethorpe—to a porn star, and then come back to an artistic theme as a model and actor. And while he was making films he was making the industry a whole load of money. And here he was, gone without a word being said.

No black performers were commemorated that year, and pretty soon I noticed no black performers were receiving awards either. Although I should have won best newcomer, I didn't. In fact, not one non-white performer received any award in the course of the entire evening, and that made me mad. I knew black movies sold. I knew that when I went in adult bookstores the white movies were soon on sale while the black movies were holding longer at full price, which meant that people were buying them. And to me it seemed nothing less than bare-faced racism that none of this was acknowledged in any way at the Probies. You have to bear in mind that this was 1997, not 1967, so there was no excuse for a lack of awareness on race issues on the part of the show's organizers.

So I sat there steaming, determined I was going to speak up and try and do something about this lack of acknowledgement. My chance came after the award ceremony was over. I got up out of my seat and went to speak to the board, the guys who represented and presented the Probies. Michael Skee, author and former gay/bi editor for AVN, was one of them, along with a bunch of other white guys from within the industry whose names I don't now recall.

Austin Black, a fellow porn star I'd made a couple of films with, and who passed away in 2006, was witness to the whole thing. He was a beefy, very light-skinned Blatino performer with a taste for leather and a masculine bearing.

I explained to the guys on the board what I didn't like about what I'd seen and heard that evening, and I guess I must have got kind of mad about it, because at one point I had one of them by the throat. Austin grabbed my arm and said, "Bobby, stop this! They gon' call the police on you!"

"Good!" I told him. "Let 'em!"

But I let go of the guy and he stumbled back looking alarmed, covering his throat with his hand and gasping for breath.

"Y'all better have this shit together for next year," I told him, looking round at Michael Skee and the rest of them. "Because this is bullshit y'all pulling, and I will not stand for it!"

And I turned on my heel, and I left.

Well, because I made that stand, the next year it was me and Chi Chi LaRue hosting the Probies, and I received an award in what was I think a new category that year, "Best Ethnic Performer." I also got a good many invitations to host other award shows subsequent to that. It didn't please me over much, however: having a non-white co-host is often just tokenism. It doesn't alter the nature of the business itself, and I wasn't just concerned with advancing Bobby Blake the individual; I wanted to improve con-ditions and open doors for all minorities within the adult industry.

This I set about doing as soon as my level of stardom made me in-demand enough to state my terms. For example: remember the gang-bang movie I mentioned a few chapters back, where shooting had to be stopped because the guy's ass was bleeding, and I said I wasn't going nowhere until I got my check? One thing that was interesting about that partic-ular episode was how the other performers, all of them black men, were prepared to accept poor treatment from the pro-ducers of that movie. They were used to it. They had been in the industry far longer than me, a lot of them, and they had been beaten down by it. But I saw no reason to put up with bullshit from anyone, regardless of their skin color or social position. I had zero tolerance for it, and I didn't care if that made me unpopular with some producers and some direc-tors and company owners.

As was typical in that kind of situation some of my fellow performers had a problem with my determination to be respected, even though by standing my ground I was attempting to raise the bar for all of us to be treated better.

"It's got to be your way or no way," they complained.

To which my reply was, "Hell, yeah."

Because by that point I'd watched some black actors kiss ass to be accepted. In doing so they established themselves as inferiors, and so the minute they stopped kissing ass to demand nothing more than reasonable treatment they got dumped. But I understood the power of the dollar: my films outsold all the other black films by a ratio of ten to one, and knowing that gave me the confidence to assert myself on the set.

I never got a bad check and I always got paid.

Sometimes some of these cheap producers wouldn't even pay their actors. Sometimes they got away with it; other times it backfired on them.

Take the year I was co-hosting the Probies: I watched this crazy drag queen beat a producer down for giving him a bad check, and I had to laugh because that producer was getting what he deserved, and in front of an audience too.

I worked hard on building myself up as a star, and I'm proud to be able to say that through that I opened some doors for other black performers. I was the first black performer to headline in a Catalina film—Paul Baressi's *Iron Cage*—and that led to Flex-Deon Blake headlining for Catalina years earlier than he would have otherwise done. I was the first black model on the cover of *Unzipped* magazine, one of the largest gay porn publications, and I made a deal with the guys who ran *Unzipped* that if that issue sold well they would put another African-American model on the cover. Now, that issue outsold every previous issue of that magazine, so the publishers were as good as their word and featured Tyson Cane on the very next cover. Unfortunately he didn't do so well for them, but still it was a breakthrough for all of us as black and non-white models and performers.

I also advanced black performers because I'd built a name for myself at a time when a lot of straight video companies were looking to produce gay films. As I had discovered from attending the AVN awards in Las Vegas they knew who I was, and so it was natural that I became the first male performer, black or white, to headline their new gay titles. My profitability encouraged those companies to use other black performers in their films when maybe otherwise they would not have done so.

My persona, which had brought me so much success, was that of a certain type of black man, an aggressive, masculine top. People have sometimes raised the issue of stereotyping with me. They ask me did I consider that I was portraying the cliché of the thuggish black stud who fucks anything that moves? And if that was the case, did it bother me?

To be honest it wasn't something I gave any thought to—it never bothered me. I liked the sort of sex I liked, and that was personal to me. I would be asked to perform in a film on the basis of the sort of sex I enjoyed, I would turn up, do my thing, and get paid, and how it was perceived and what the viewer put onto it I didn't worry about. If you worry about how you're perceived then you're not going to be able to do your job effectively.

But if I was going to think about it, then I would say this: if you're performing in an orgy where all the participants are black men, and some are fucking and some are being fucked, some are sucking and rimming and some are being sucked and rimmed, and some are doing all of those things and more, then on an overall basis that film isn't stereotyping of black men.

Another obvious question I'll deal with here is with all the films I was making in such a short period—more than twenty a year—was I worried about being over-exposed? As with the issue of stereotyping, again the answer is no: I was offered work, I took it, and I got paid well for doing it. I didn't worry much about over-exposure because I sought to raise my game with every movie I made: with every performance I tried to make sure that I did something I had never done on film before, or said something I had never said before, so there was something new for the viewer to get off on.

Where I did make sure not to get over-exposed was in person. For instance: if I went to a nude beach, as I did now and again, then I would make sure to keep a thong on. My reasoning on that was simple and straightforward: if guys could see it all for free, why would they pay to buy a magazine or rent a film? For similar reasons I stopped dancing or stripping unless I was headlining an event, say at Man Country up in Chicago, or The Campus, over in San Francisco. I wanted seeing Bobby Blake in person to be a special experience for my fans. And finally I retired from making films at the top of my game, which is the ultimate way to avoid being over-exposed!

In some respects my rising fame constrained my life. For instance, at one point when I was in Los Angeles I decided to join Bally's gym, which is a very nice gym high up in the Hollywood Hills, spacious, well-equipped, and high-tech. Now, when I go to the gym I don't go to play; I'm not looking to meet anybody. I've never done that my entire life. I go to work out and leave.

Well, the first time I drive up there I present my card at the reception desk, and even though the card is in my real name the manager recognizes me and says, "Oh, I love your movies."

So you know what? I just turned right back around and left.

And when I got home I called and cancelled my membership. And the reason I did that was that I had to have some personal space, and the manager's attitude made me realize Bally's was nothing but a gay gym, full of guys cruising and looking to hook up.

Now, I don't mind being recognized: that will happen from time to time wherever you go. But I just didn't want to be trying to exercise in an environment where sex was such a focal point.

So that was one downside of fame. But on the whole life was good. I got to drive luxury cars and hang out with mainstream stars. At one point I was spending three thousand dollars a day shopping and at the same time putting money aside against the future and supporting my family. I felt like

I was doing what I wanted and I was in the place I wanted to be. I had no doubts, nor any feeling that what I was doing was in any way wrong.

I do believe that a big part of the reason I felt that way about doing porn was because in the view of many people, particularly those in the black Church, being gay puts you outside of respectable society anyway. Though I am bi-sexual, when I am involved with another man I am treated as gay, so that same judgment falls on me as a bisexual man: I am oftentimes placed outside respectable society. Now, for a straight person to step over into the adult film business, they are passing from the world of respectability into what is seen as a world of sin. That's a big step to take, especially if you're a woman. You're shifting from approval to disapproval. But for a gay man the move is from being seen as one kind of sinner to being seen as another kind of sinner, so it feels like a much smaller kind of step. And that's part of why I found it easy to enter the world of adult entertainment.

Also, I was good at it, and finding that you're good at something is very seductive. So is being in demand for what you can do well. We all want to be wanted.

Another thing that was very important to me was that I had a lot of good people around me. Not just directors like Edward James, but many of the guys I performed with. Porn actors are stereotyped as flakey, damaged individuals with alcohol and substance abuse problems, losers on downward trajectories towards the gutter or the grave. Of course that's true of some of them, probably more than the average, but others are decent, kind people with integrity and focus. It's about some of those people I want to talk next.

CHAPTER TWENTY-ONE:

CO-WORKERS

Over time Edward James, who was the director I worked with most often, and with whom I had the closest relationship, built up a team of actors he preferred to use. Of course I was one of those actors. I also had strong opinions about who I best liked to work with, and between the two of us we put together a kind of family of porn stars who were to appear regularly in most of the films I made during my three years' involvement in the industry. Anyone who's seen any of my movies—which will be most of you reading this book— will recognize the names Bam, Kevin Kemp, Richard Reyes, Ricky Parker, J. C. Carter, and Flex-Deon Blake. Other guys came and went, but they were probably the main six. Bam, Kevin Kemp, and Flex-Deon were my rivals, and I'll talk about them in the next chapter. Richard, Ricky, and J. C. were the guys I most often had sex with on-camera.

I'd say I had choice of who I worked with about 97% of the time. Less so at first, of course, but as my fame increased I could increasingly control who I worked with. The performers I preferred to have in the films with me were the ones who had no attitude and were easy to work with, guys like Ricky Parker and J. C. Carter. I needed guys who could just take it—I'm not one to have any patience when I'm fucking a guy, with him complaining that it hurts and telling me I have to stop. My attitude is, I'm hard and I'm gonna shove my dick in and you should be ready. Ricky Parker in particular was always ready for what was needed.

One time we were shooting this movie on Santa Monica Boulevard. We'd been working all morning and we were taking a break. There was me, Edward James, Ricky Parker and some of the other guys, sitting outside at this restaurant eating pizza.

For those few of you who don't know, Ricky's a dark-skinned, boyish guy, maybe 5'7", with a shaved head and usually a shaved body, who's often billed in reviews as a "super-bottom." I heard he once did a film where he was a top, but mostly he's into being fucked. He gets real vocal, real excited when a dick's up him. The hardest fuck I ever gave him was probably in the party movie *Dogbone*. Anyway, there we were at this pizza place eating and drinking Cokes and bullshitting, you know, and Edward James leans over and says to me, "I dare you to make Ricky suck your dick right here, right out on the street."

Now, this was lunch-time and in broad daylight, but I just turned to Edward James and said, "Watch." Then I turned to Ricky and said, "You know what you got to do. Get on your knees and suck my dick." And I pushed my chair back from the table a little ways and unzipped my fly. Now, this is

Ricky Parker also an idiot beggin along w/ the others [illegible] command they gone [illegible] in his self-esteem

the kind of guy Ricky is: without any further prompting he put down his pizza, took a sip of Coke, wiped his mouth, got down on his knees and went down on me.

We were kind of screened by the table, but not really. One woman walked by twice with her poodle, just goggling at what was going on. I guess even in West Hollywood she wasn't used to seeing a guy getting his dick sucked by another guy right out in the open.

The poodle started barking, which is when I took in that this woman was watching us, so I pulled Ricky's mouth off my dick and gestured for him to get up and sit back down while I zipped back up. Then we carried on with our meal.

Now, that happened because Edward James dared me, and I've always liked doing things that people would dare me not to. But it's also a perfect example of what made Ricky so easy to work with: he just did what was required of him. *Asshole statement*

So much for sticking up for others Richard Reyes was another porn star I enjoyed working with. 99% of the time he took my dick without complaint. He's a lean, handsome, shaven-headed blatino guy with kind of the look of Prince about him. He's well-endowed but usually plays a bottom in movies: he was named Tom of Finland's Butt-Boy of the Year in 1996 and was the star of the white-on-black gang-bang movie *Black Hole*. He played my boyfriend in *Soul Patrol*, where I play a police officer, and we made a number of orgy films together, like *Black Leather Gang-Bang* and *High Rollin', a Black Thang*. He was versatile in *High Rollin'*, as he was in several of our films, though of course he always bottomed when he was with me.

Richard's also bisexual, which I didn't realize until I

starred alongside him in the bi film *Goldilocks and the Three Bi-Bears*. In the scene we did together he surprised me by fucking that girl just as hard as I did! He's a fine, good-looking man, but like so many in the industry he lost his focus and never became as big a star as he might have done. My first-ever porn partner, Gene LaMarr, also appeared in *Goldilocks and the Three Bi-Bears*, which was my favorite of the bisexual films I made.

I didn't always enjoy them, though. I'm happy to fuck women but I need them to be well-presented, and there have been times when the ladies would arrive at the shoot looking any old way. They would turn up looking like hell and then they'd start putting these wigs on their damn heads, pile on the makeup, glue on the false eyelashes and all that kind of stuff right in front of me. And I would send 'em home because my philosophy was: you doing a film with me then you come with that shit already on, because that transformation is a complete turn-off to me. I didn't want to see these women arrive looking a mess, then doing all that work to look a little bit better, because I would remember when they looked a mess, and be turned all the way off. To add insult to injury they'd still get the majority of the money, because the focus was more on them than on the men, which is why, as I've already mentioned, I never did straight movies.

I did do a bisexual movie with Ricky Parker—*Bi Bi Black*—where he and this lady, I think it was Kitten, competed to get to suck my dick. That was kind of fun. But Ricky was never bisexual that I recall.

My favorite of all the guys I worked with—by which I

mean the guys I fucked rather than the other tops that were in the film alongside me—was undoubtedly J. C. Carter. I've always said I would never date somebody who did porn, and that I could never fall in love with somebody who did porn, (Flex-Deon I fell in love with before he became involved in the adult industry; it was through me that he started making adult films). I had this firm belief that I couldn't fall in love with a fellow porn star, and that was because I always viewed sex with other porn actors as a job. I removed myself emotionally from the sex, switching myself off and becoming Bobby Blake the Porn Star, throwing myself into using and humiliating whoever I was fucking, calling them all kinds of bitches, having fun making them holler and scream, then picking up a paycheck at the end of the day.

With J. C. Carter I felt differently: from the first moment I met him this guy was just totally beautiful—mentally, physically—just overall beautiful. He's my best friend today, and I love him with all my body, my spirit, and soul. And as a colleague I applaud him because he's always been about business. For those of you who don't know him, he's light-skinned, maybe 5'9", compact, extremely buff, kind of boyish and clean-shaven, and has a big sun tattoo on one shoulder.

Our first encounter I do kind of regret, though.

It was on the set of the Paul Barresi *Iron Cage* movie. J. C., who I didn't know at all then, made a comment that made me so mad I fucked him so hard in that movie he had to go to the doctor. I did it on purpose, and to this day he doesn't know that. After we were done he said, "Bobby, you did

Why is such sick sarcasm being channelled as show a normal reaction to insults whata disgusting man

something to me," and I didn't say nothing, just nodded.

That was the downright nasty side of me: if I heard some-one on a shoot had said something unpleasant about me, I would specifically tell the producer, "I want that person in a scene with me." They wouldn't even know I had arranged it that way. And I would dog them out and try and send them to the hospital.

With J. C., what it was, he had made some remark that made me feel he was putting down black men in general. He was in a relationship with a white guy, and I felt that he did-n't date black guys, and it made me mad, so that's why I did, what I did. *No -excuse— you're a sick bastard.*

Actually, though, if I'm honest, a big part of it was that I wanted him but I couldn't have him because he was in this relationship with this other guy, regardless of whether the guy was black or white or whatever.

Later I came to find out that J. C. wasn't putting black men down, but that was after the fact. So, J. C., if you're reading these pages, I apologize wholeheartedly for what I did to you on *Iron Cage*.

J. C. and me, we speak practically every day. We talk about things in the porn industry, we share our experiences, our likes and dislikes, and what's deepest in our hearts. He's back in school like I am, working on a degree in criminal jus-tice. He wants to go into law enforcement, I think. He's been in a relationship for the last four years with a guy from Spain, and I've been to visit them, and he's come to visit me.

J. C. may not be as tall as I am, but he's a strong guy and like me he has a zero tolerance for bullshit. I was once visiting Chicago, and J. C. and I were doing a show with Man Country, an appearance at a club. We got a cab from the airport and the driver had just taken us all over the world before he took us to the club. Now, J. C. is from Chicago and he knew perfectly well what the driver had been doing, so when the guy asked us for forty dollars J. just shook his head and said, "Look, here's fifteen."

"No," the driver said. "Forty."

"Look, man," J. C. said, "I'm from here. You took this damn cab all over the goddamn world. If you don't take this money you won't get shit. You won't get nothing but an ass-whipping!"

And he looked at the guy like, take it or nothing, and the man took the money and left. And I thought, "Wow! This li'l motherfucker, he's tough!" He's nice, but like me he's not going to be pushed around. And J. C.'s been very successful in the industry, and built a name for himself, which is harder to do if you're known as a bottom. So he's one of a kind, and I love him to death. My best friend, J. C. Carter.

By the by, don't ever think that I have anything less than total respect for passive guys. I love fucking, and I love guys who are into getting fucked. If I'm talking about hurtin' and humiliatin' that's a performance thing: it's not about disrespecting a guy because he enjoys taking dick. That would make no sense. The one thing I don't like is guys acting girly. It turns me off sexually, and I think it loses you the respect of the wider community.

Now, if I loved J. C. Carter as a friend, my best friend in the business, the man I fell most deeply and devastatingly in love with was Flex-Deon Blake. Flex and I were lovers for four years, during which time we made over a dozen films together. I gave him my last name and we were known as a celebrity porn couple. We never had sex with each other on film—that was the line we drew to maintain some privacy in our relationship—but we fucked other guys together, we put on shows together, and for a short time we even escorted together. Of all the people I worked with in the adult entertainment business he was unquestion ably the most significant to me. I'm going to talk about my relationship with him more fully later on, but in the next chapter I want to talk about my rivals: Bam, Kevin Kemp, and Tiger Tyson.

CHAPTER TWENTY-TWO:

RIVALS

Any other black tops who knew how to throw down I saw as my rivals in the movie business. This may sound harsh, but even my lover, Flex-Deon, became a rival when we were on-set together and competing to see who could fuck ass the hardest and longest. Other pretenders to the crown were to come along during my time in the industry, guys like Tiger Tyson, but my main rivals were my fellow actors with Bacchus: Bam and Kevin Kemp. Both of them I saw as threats because they had bigger dicks than me, and in porn as in the rest of life, size counts.

Of the two of them, Bam was unquestionably the more striking-looking. He was 6', lean, dark, tattooed, with a thuggish shaved head, a nose-stud and a goatee, and a dick that was thick around and at least twelve inches long. Kevin Kemp was fit, well-groomed with a small, neatly-trimmed moustache, and had more of a boyish, clean-cut preppy look, which was also popular with the fans. He, too, had a huge dick, and on a performance level I considered him more of a threat because he could maintain a hard-on, which Bam mostly couldn't do.

Kevin Kemp was less promoted as a personality than either Bam or myself within the industry—or worked less hard to promote himself—but he certainly got his share of box-covers. And box-cover presence is an obvious measurement of how highly a performer is thought of, so I had to take notice of him.

I watched Kevin Kemp closely and my conclusion was that because our personal styles were so different we weren't really in competition with each other. Sure, we were both tops, and we were both African-American men working in the gay porn business, but fans of my performances wanted something very different from what Kevin Kemp had to offer. Bam was more of a threat to me because what he was doing was closer to what I was doing.

There were two approaches I took to Bam. One was to build up the rivalry between us, which I did both in print interviews and through things I would say about him in my films. Director Edward James colluded in this because it built both me and Bam up as stars, and that was good for him, and for Bacchus as well.

The most obvious example of my trash-talking would be at the start of the film *Bam*, which is obviously intended to be a star vehicle for Bam, and features only him and no one else on the box-cover.

The film begins not with him, however, but with a ten-minute monologue that consists of me talking directly to the camera, with Edward James firing me up with questions from behind the lens and encouraging me to mouth off.

I talk trash about how bitches like whoever's watching the movie right now are out there turning tricks for me and making me the money to buy the house we're filming in. I'm acting out a kind of pimp persona, making out I'm all about the benjamins, and just generally bragging. But I also tell it like it is—I say that Bam is a bottom because he can't get a hard-on without a finger up the ass, that he's lazy at fucking, and I end with an invitation to the viewer: "You watch and you decide. Is he a top? Or is he a bottom?"

Now Edward James filmed that interview after we shot the movie, so you can guess what he thinks about Bam's performance from the fact that he edited it so it was right at the start.

So just at that moment when Bam was getting top billing I was there taking him down.

Talking up our rivalry built both of us up and froze Kevin Kemp out. It was no accident that *Black Inches* regularly featured me and Bam in its pages, or that the publishers regarded it as a coup when they got us to do a photo shoot together. They never did that with Kevin Kemp.

I was also keen to do scenarios with Bam, where he and I would take it in turns to fuck various guys. That was my second approach to dealing with him: create a situation where we were in direct competition with each other. So in *Bam* we double-team with J. C. Carter at the film's climax, and at the beginning with an accommodating, boyish African-American bottom named Craig Stevens. I wanted viewers to see how my dick was rock-hard while Bam's was flabby, and

I wanted them to see me dog guys out and make them holler while Bam's ass-fucking was lackluster. I wanted the contrast to be right there in front of your eyes.

At some points I even went further, taking charge of the situation, telling Bam to fuck Craig harder, grabbing his ass to make him pump his hips faster against Craig's butt. You watch those scenes and you can see in those scenes he doesn't manage to assert his personality against mine, and that's how I wanted it.

Another thing in my favor when it came to dealing with Bam was basic smarts: like a lot of my fellow porn actors Bam had no business sense. I found that out when he came to me during a movie shoot and said, "Bobby, All Worlds wants to make a dildo of my dick."

"Great," I said. "How much are you getting paid?"

He shrugged and got the contract out of his bag and handed it to me. I took my time and read it over carefully and it all seemed legit until I came to the bit where the amount of money Bam was supposed to be paid was specified and it was a blank line. They wanted him to sign the contract without the money being decided.

"Bam," I said, "you can't sign this."

"Why not?"

"Because once you sign it they could just write "three dollars" on this line and that's all you'd get. You'd just be in the bad."

He nodded and took the contract back off of me.

I came to find out later he went behind my back and signed it anyway, and in the end they gave him a hundred dollars. All Worlds was mad when it heard I'd told him not to sign—they didn't like anyone standing up to them. But I thought it was wrong for them to take advantage of him, and even though Bam was my rival he was a brother and someone had to look after my people.

I had one final advantage over Bam: I wanted it more. Bam was basically heterosexual—he even made a few straight porn movies—but did gay porn for the money. That's part of why a lot of his performances aren't that good. When he wasn't filming he was off partying and chasing pussy. He wasn't really that ambitious; he was just a man who happened to have a foot-long dick. So however much his agent and the studios and directors would try and build him up it never amounted to anything that impressive.

The technique I used with Bam I also used in the numerous gang-bang movies I starred in, from *High Rollin', a G Thang* to *Dog Bone*: take control of the situation, take charge, and then throw down a performance that would make sure the camera was on me as often as possible for as much of the time as possible. In those sorts of situations noisy, enthusiastic bottoms like Ricky Parker were an asset because they were attention-getting.

I had a concept that I could always outshine the person who was next to me—I was always going to do or say something they weren't expecting from me. And because I was such a dependable performer I could exert influence and generally control how I was filmed as well as controlling who I worked with and what I did.

So that was how I saw off both Bam and Kevin Kemp.

Not having an agent I was free to make deals they were unable to make, and I managed to command higher fees than either of them for appearing in films. I think that their agents actually held them back in some respects: they had a view of their clients that was limited in a way that my view of myself was not.

The next serious contender for the title of number one black top was Tiger Tyson, and I took him very seriously indeed. He was a handsome, biracial Puerto-Rican/African-American, street-styled, well-hung, and an aggressive ass-fucker who had no problems keeping it hard. He was hungry for success, and ambitious to get to the top. He was younger than me, and so he gave the impression of being one of a new generation, keen to force their elders to step aside and shuffle off to the glue factory. That's my expression for where sex performers are sent once they're used up and worn out, like old racehorses. But you can believe I wasn't heading for no damn glue factory!

Tiger Tyson was promoted to stardom by a director-producer named Enrique Cruz. Enrique Cruz didn't operate under the umbrella of any major gay production company. His gimmick was to shoot his movies more like rap videos, using surprising camera angles and different formats, so some bits would be shot in widescreen, some would be black-and-white and so on, and the soundtrack would be more street-level and hip than was usual in gay movies. *Off Da Hook*, the film of his that most stands out, has Tiger Tyson recording a rap at a sound studio before getting down to fucking with the sound engineer and others. Enrique

Cruz was a shrewd promoter, especially to the African-American community, and it dawned on me pretty rapidly that Tiger Tyson was becoming extremely popular with my core audience.

I was alarmed but I could see this would be another great rivalry, and if I was smart it could promote my image still further.

My first move was to challenge Tiger Tyson—on tape—to do a film alongside me. I challenged him a number of times but he never responded. That was kind of a victory for me, but still I was concerned: still he was popular.

Then came a time when I was booked, along with Flex-Deon, to do a show at a Gay Pride event in Detroit, Michigan. When we arrived I discovered that Tiger Tyson and the other guys from Enrique Cruz's studio had been booked to do a show as well, and they were going on right before us. Now, that was good because we were still getting top billing, but as you can imagine I watched their show with considerable attention, keen to see what they would deliver. And you know what? I was relieved.

When I saw Tiger Tyson and the other guys in person the first thing that struck me was that they were all small. They were also less good-looking than they were in their films, which bore out my own personal philosophy about refusing to wear make-up in my films or for the box-cover shoots, because that way when people see me I always look exactly like I look on the screen. People even say I look better in real life, which is always nice to hear. Anyway, Tiger Tyson and the rest of 'em looked rough, with bad skin. And I looked down and saw they were dancing in dirty tennis shoes. Their choreography was nothing, and they just came across to me and the crowd as tacky-looking and unprofessional.

Right then and there I knew Tiger Tyson wasn't going to climb over me, and shortly after that he faded away into the sunset. Supposedly he retired in 1999, but then he was back in 2002 with his own production company. Then he "retired" in 2004, but straight away started making films with a company named Pitbull Productions. I don't know how together a person he really is, but I will say in his favor that he openly supports gay rights and AIDS research, which some performers who profit from the gay dollar do not.

There wasn't any rival who I didn't face down during the time I made adult films. I was smarter than any of them, and I could outsmart all of them. The rivalry that was most painful and difficult, and which brought me to the most serious personal crisis of my life, was with my then-partner, Flex-Deon Blake.

He talks of a rivalry but there is all in his head as at no point in time can he pinpoint how there they were in competition.

CHAPTER TWENTY-THREE:

BLATINO

Before I talk about Flex-Deon I should talk about the Blatino sex party scene I got involved with while I was in the adult film business, and which I went on being involved with for a few years after I retired from making films, because it was at a Blatino event that I first met Flex.

Now at that time I had a play-son named 'Dennis'. I don't have any biological sons, as far as I know, but I do have a number of play-sons. These are younger black gay men to whom I have become a kind of mentor or father-figure. I originally met Dennis through Steve Johnson, the guy I worked on *Whassup* magazine with and did AIDS prevention and information outreach work in Oakland for, and we became very close.

Blatino was run out of New York by a group called A-1 Black Elite, and Dennis was involved with them. As I was an increasingly famous black gay porn star, Dennis invited me to come on board with them. This I was happy to do as it had the potential to make me a lot of money. It would also give me the chance to further promote myself as a porn star, as it would be natural for me to host the parties we would throw.

I was granted what amounted to a franchise to use the Blatino name to run sex parties on the West Coast, while the A-1 guys would continue to run them on the East coast. That way we would be building brand in a way that would benefit all of us, while at the same time avoiding treading on each other's toes.

On the West Coast we actually ran two separate sorts of events: Blatino, which was for black and latino guys only, and Ariba, which was for men of all colors. Ariba events we ran mostly in Los Angeles, Blatino in L. A., Atlanta, Chicago and Washington, and both Blatino and Ariba parties were popular and successful.

The observant among you will have noticed that Washington is on the East Coast, which didn't endear me to the founders of the Blatino scene. Let me explain how that came to happen.

The East Coast guys were successful, but not very professional. I did what I have done throughout my life: I observed how they ran things and worked out how I could improve on it. I brought professionalism and a tough-minded desire to succeed to bear on what I was doing. I was aggressive in promoting events. I brought in porn stars like J. C. Carter to add glamour and star power.

Above all, just as I had at Greater Mount Pleasant back in Memphis, in a very different context, I brought organ-ization. We hired hotel suites. We sold tickets in advance at gay venues. We had strict rules and regulations, and we had monitors in every room to ensure they were adhered to.

The party itself would be off the chain—maybe a thousand guys just having sex, sex, sex—and we wanted everyone to have fun. But we had security on the door who let you know that no meant no, that no violence of any sort would be tolerated, and that anyone caught having unsafe sex would be thrown out.

That safe sex educational aspect was always very important to me. It made what we were doing somehow reputable and responsible, even if what we were doing was arranging sex parties.

Where the discipline and organization really made the difference was that we never once got busted. We didn't tolerate guys wandering around in the hotel hallways, for instance, or hanging around outside the hotel. I was very much, "If you got a ticket, come in, if you don't, leave."

The guys in New York were less disciplined, and their parties got busted by the police several times, which was obviously bad for business and their reputation. Who wants to go to a gay orgy and have the cops come kicking in the door and taking names and addresses?

The first year I hosted the Blatino party we threw it at the Mid-Town Spa, which is a large club in L. A. It was packed, and there was a long line at the door. Another party we threw in Atlanta—me, J. C., and a bunch of other porn stars—had a thousand people in there and we turned away carloads more. I would say we turned away six or seven hundred people that night—it was just unbelievable how successful it was. And we had wild sex, just laid out on the floor, training it until we couldn't go no more.

The word of mouth was great, and people would come from all over the country to attend our events. A few rivals sprang up, but they were never as well organized or successful as us, so they never worried me. West Coast Blatino became a phenomenon in itself, and since I'm a southern boy it felt natural to take it across to Washington, D.C. which, since Washington is on the Eastern seaboard, was when I became unpopular with the founders of Blatino. But I didn't care. I was all about making money, and that was it, I didn't ask for any permission; I just did it. *Typical of this crass asshole.*

In D. C. we hired the presidential suite, which took up the whole floor of the hotel. It was vast, like a cathedral, and as I recall we charged everyone who attended thirty-five dollars admission. The hotel staff were cool with it because we never gave them any reason to come up to the floor we'd hired during the event unless we were calling on them to do something specific, and we policed ourselves carefully. I managed to patch things up sufficiently with the East Coast group that they were prepared to be involved with throwing the party. The bottom line was that since they knew it would be a success, getting involved was the smart and profitable thing for them to do. But it was very much my event: my organization, planning, and promotion.

It's the sort of work that burns you out, though.

When I hosted parties people came on to me constantly. And when I found someone I wanted to interact with more personally, or in private, it was impossible. I got tired, everyone involved got tired, because there was a lot of pressure on all of us—the hosts, the security teams—to make sure that everybody was safe, to make sure everyone was having a nice time, to keep things monitored. Plus, I would go to every Black Gay Pride event, starting with Splash, in Houston, Texas, which was on every year in May, and was the first Pride of the year, and then on to Washington, which was a huge event, and on and on, and I would just get totally drained. I was meeting so many people and handshaking and trying to be friendly to everyone, networking and doing public relations both as Bobby Blake, porn star, and Bobby Blake, host and promoter of Blatino parties, that I became exhausted. There was just so much business going on, a lot more business than pleasure.

Eventually it reached a point where I just wasn't enjoying it any more—it had taken over my life. It was running me, I wasn't running it. So I withdrew from the Blatino scene and let others carry it on. But before I stepped down I gave Edward James the rights to go ahead and use the name in a couple of movies. That would be the one time I played a role as a porn producer—organizing things behind the cameras. I appeared in both of them—*Blatino LA* and *Blatino Beach Party*, (in which I fucked both J. C. Carter and Ricky Parker, and in which Richard Reyes appeared), and they were both big sellers.

It was at one of the very first Blatino parties I hosted that I met Flex-Deon.

CHAPTER TWENTY-FOUR:

A SHOWBIZ MARRIAGE

Flex and I were without question the most famous couple in gay porn. Not only were we both porn stars as well as romantic partners, we also performed in films together, which was pretty much unique in gay adult films. We never had sex with each other on-camera, but we would fuck other guys together.

To be a couple making adult films together was newsworthy and gained both of us attention. We were interviewed and did photo shoots for *Black Inches* magazine separately and as a couple, and we were invited to do guest appearances at Pride events and put on shows all across the country as a couple.

As I've mentioned I gave Flex my last name to raise his profile and give him opportunities he would either never have had or would have had to work for many years to get, such as working with Catalina, which was and is the premiere gay porn production company.

Because Flex took my surname it was widely assumed we were married. In fact we never were, the reason being that I don't believe in gay marriage.

Now, you may ask why someone who clearly sees himself as the equal of anyone would be opposed to gay marriage. Well, there are a variety of reasons why I'm opposed, some straightforward, others less so. But I want to say right off that I believe absolutely in the right of anyone to have the sexual and emotional life he or she wants to have behind closed doors, providing it's consensual and respon-sible and adult.

I don't like gay marriage being pushed as a political agenda. It's extremely unpopular amongst the wider African-American community. As an African-American I don't like being pressured to sign up to any agenda by a gay rights movement that has always been predominantly white, and has historically shown next to no interest in the rights of its fellow black gay men and women. And for myself I feel that there are more important issues that need sorting out first—the seemingly deeply-rooted inability of gay men, particular-ly black gay men, to commit to each other, for instance.

When I was a dancer I was struck by how often couples would watch me perform. I would be up there at the Uptown Downtown or wherever, dancing, putting on a show and enjoying myself. These guys would give me and the other dancers tips, and that was nice, of course, and there was to my mind nothing wrong with them showing their appreciation of my physique and my performance. But then one half of the couple would sneak back to the club the following night or the following week and try to pick me up, try to get me to have sex with him behind his mate's back.

I would always remember them from the previous night, or the previous week, and say, "But aren't you in a relationship?"

"Yes, but he doesn't understand me," was the standard reply. "He can't give me what I need." So there they were, coming on to me.

Now, I'm not saying heterosexual couples are without their troubles, Lord knows. But it seems to me that the less overtly political issue of male couples being able to establish loving, faithful relationships between each other through commitment and communication is more important than that of gay marriage.

Maybe I'm a cynic when it comes to marriage anyway. Marriage is only an outward symbol, after all. The papers, the marriage certificate, the lavish wedding ceremony, the exchange of rings weighed down with so many carats—all these are just outward symbols. They're supposed to be saying, "I love this person." The ring is supposed to declare that I want to be with this person through the ups and the downs, good times and bad. But experience has taught me that if it's not in the heart then I don't care how many rings you put on your finger. I don't care how many times you stand up and declare you want to be with this person for a lifetime. It means nothing.

The fact of the matter is that, even with all these extravagant symbols, divorce rates among straight couples are at an all-time sky-high. Why would I imagine that being able to marry would help me sustain my loving partnership in any way?

But whatever the arguments my personal bottom line is, I'm not going to stand before the God of Abraham, Isaac, and Jacob and tell him I want to marry another man. I'm just not going to do it. And that's just about me, and what I'm comfortable with. I'm not ashamed of being bisexual. I don't believe it's wrong for me to desire and love another man. But I also don't believe it's necessary for me to marry a man to express that desire and love for him. And I will not be co-opted into supporting agendas pushed forward by groups who don't support me.

So Flex and myself, we were never married. But we did love each other. I loved him with a great intensity, and for three years he was my significant other.

For the first of those years it was a perfect relationship, but then things began to go wrong. Things began to happen that were eventually to bring me to the lowest point of my entire life.

People see Bobby Blake as this big, strong warrior figure. That was how I saw myself, and that was how I wanted to be seen. But there was a time in my life when events really humbled me, stripped me of my sense of myself, and came close to robbing me of both my faith and my sanity. And that was during my relationship with Flex.

I first met Flex when I was hosting the first West Coast Blatino party, at the Mid-Town Spa in L. A. I was passing out flyers outside a club on Wilshire Boulevard called Club Boy and I gave him one because he was just so gorgeous—a shaven-headed, flawlessly dark-skinned, masculine African-American male with a smooth, body-builder's physique and an amazing, rock-hard butt.

I gave him a flyer and he came to the party and we talked a little, and we flirted, and we slipped into a private room for a few minutes. We didn't do more than kiss and hug at that time, however, because I was the host and couldn't be away from my duties for long, and we couldn't meet up after the party because I was flying straight out to Chicago to host another Blatino party there.

For some reason Flex and I didn't exchange numbers, and on the plane out to Chicago I was thinking, "Damn, I want to see that fine-ass brother again. I fucked that up."

But business is business, I was known for hosting big parties, it was my job, and you don't let people down.

The next time I met Flex was in Washington, over Memorial Day weekend, about three months later. He came to the party I was hosting there. That was the one that the East Coast Blatino guys got pissed about. J. C. Carter was guesting, and we had over a thousand people crowded in that hotel suite having fun. Flex gave me his phone number and told me where he was staying. But you know what? I threw the number away. I never called him. There were so many fine brothers all around me that I just wasn't thinking about him. So I just let that go.

The following weekend I was back in L. A. A friend of mine who knew Flex came by and said, "Look, dude, this dude has been axing about you. He know we know each other. Is it okay if I give him your number?"

I said, "Sure."

So he gave Flex my number and Flex hit me up and we started talking. We talked and talked and talked, so despite the fact that we had found each other extremely physically attractive what got our relationship going wasn't sex but sharing deeply personal things in words.

In many respects we also shared a background. We were both masculine-type bisexual African-American men who had grown up in the South. We were both brought up in traditional Christian households where church-going, spirituality and faith were important. And despite our sexuality and our involvement in the adult entertainment industry neither of us had rejected the faith of our childhoods.

Unlike me, Flex grew up in a two-parent household. He had three sisters. After high school he joined the United States Air Force and served his country for thirteen years, traveling the world and living for periods in Italy, Greece, and Japan. He had always loved music, so following his time in the military he went to college and studied piano.

It was around that time that his world began to darken. He quit college to be nearer to his parents, whose health was beginning to fail, moving to Miami, becoming a corrections officer and a Minister of Music at a local church, where he played organ, piano, and directed a number of choirs. Two years later his parents both passed away within three months of each other, which was clearly deeply painful for him.

Shortly after that Flex entered the world of adult gay entertainment, which had always fascinated him. He became involved in the porn biz at a point where he was both bearing that burden of grief and, paradoxically, when he knew that he would never have to worry that his parents might find out about it. He was at that time married to a woman, and had kids. That relationship had floundered, the couple had separated, and there were ongoing problems with child support issues at the time I met him.

So he shared these things about himself with me, and I shared things about myself and my early life. After a couple of weeks I went down to visit him in Miami and things went very well. We talked about what we wanted from a relationship and decided we agreed we shared the same goals. We had the same ideas about what our relationship would mean, and we committed to following them through.

Having a long-distance relationship soon became very expensive, and of course it's not a satisfactory way of conducting a relationship whether money is an issue or not. So I decided to give up my home in Los Angeles and move to Florida. Flex and I leased a place together in Pembroke Pines, in a new-ish upscale subdivision forty-five minutes' drive from South Beach.

And that was that perfect first year.

CHAPTER TWENTY-FIVE:

ME AND
MARILYN MONROE

Flex wanted into the adult film business. He wanted it bad. And since it was something I was doing very successfully, and at the time enjoyed doing, I saw no reason to stand in his way. In fact I helped him pretty much every way I could—I gave him my name, I introduced him to people, and I gave him advice about how to manage himself and his career.

However, even though he was my lover, when Flex was working in adult films, because his performing persona was, like mine, that of a top, he was also my rival. When we made films together, once the camera started rolling, Kevin and Edgar disappeared and were replaced by Flex-Deon Blake and Bobby Blake.

While filming I did what I always did—threw down as memorable a performance as I could in the hope that the viewer would forget the other guy was even there. I support-

ed Flex behind the scenes, but in front of the camera it's
every man for himself. *So much for love?*

The fact that I knew Flex could be promoted as a rival to
me meant that I was careful not to tell him all my secrets. I
didn't give him all my contacts. I didn't share all my insights
with him. Some things he would have to learn by himself.

Partly that was me protecting my own interests, but part
of it was my belief in hard work and discipline—that you
should earn what you have, not be given it on a plate. But
Flex was my lover, and while I looked out for myself I loved
him and wanted him to do well and be as good at what he
was doing as he could possibly be.

One thing that was always real important to me was to
divide my porn persona from my true self. It was a form of
self-protection. On stage I was violent and abusive and all
about the fucking. Offstage I was a loving, caring, sharing
individual. In front of the camera I was a total top; in my
personal life, although I had never enjoyed being fucked
when younger, I was concerned for the satisfaction of my
partner and could be somewhat broader. And that's how I
was with Flex.

All I would say against myself in terms of the way I acted
within our relationship is that I could be somewhat controlling, being as I had zero tolerance for certain kinds of behav-
iors such as drug or alcohol abuse. But if I was in any way
controlling I was always giving as well. As a small for
instance, each year we were together I threw a party for Flex's
birthday. I'd hire a suite overlooking the ocean, invite a big

crowd of our friends, and I would give him a ring inset with a diamond, one carat for each year of our relationship. Whenever I was away working, on my return I'd always bring Flex a gift bag, so he would know I loved and appreciated him.

Truth to tell, I was the financial mainstay during the entire time we were together, picking up more of the bills than I initially realized I was doing.

It was difficult for Flex to deal with my popularity, especially as we were in the same line of work. There were plenty of times when we had gone out together and somebody would come up to me who knew me from my films. They'd say, "Hey Bobby, how you doin'?" Then they'd walk on by, not acknowledging Flex, who was standing right by me.

I would call them back and say, "Come here, man. I appreciate you speaking to me, but this is my lover right here: speak to him likewise," because I demanded respect for my mate as well as myself.

The minute you let people interact with you any kind of way they want to it begins to demolish what you're trying to build. And I could see it was hard on Flex to be in that situation, especially as he was so ambitious for himself.

Flex's ambition led him into contradictory situations and mentalities to my way of thinking. I believed in elevating myself by building respect. He believed in a version of doing-whatever-it-takes-to-get-famous that I had problems with.

For instance, guys would pass by and pat him on his ass and he wouldn't be bothered. I'd say, "Flex, why you let him pat-pat on your ass?"

His response would be, "You have to expect that, we're in the porn business." He thought I was jealous that other men were touching him but it wasn't that; for me the issue was respect.

Weird he told older respectful for his 'porn-
essum, but humiliate Ricky Parker.

"You're not making a movie right now," I told him. "Let that go on and you won't get respect. And in the long run you're gon' fail. See, you have to draw the line, my brother, or people gon' look at you as if you a piece of trash."

It was the same story when we went to the nude beach together down in Florida. He would take all his clothes off even though I would always tell him not to for the business-minded reason that people won't pay to see something if they can get it for free. He was pleasing himself, but sometimes you need to put your career ahead of doing what you want on a whim.

One telling difference between the two of us was our approach to outside sex, and that surfaced most markedly when it came to escorting. I'll talk more about that in a later chapter, but there was one particular series of situations that revealed the cracks that were beginning to develop in our relationship and showed our very different outlooks on life.

First off, at the end of that first year during which I thought things had been going real well, Flex came to me and said, "I've been living a lie."

"What do you mean?" I asked.

"I've been doing things the way you want me to do," he said. "I want more freedom." He wanted to do threesomes, that kind of thing. To be honest I wasn't comfortable with it. When I'm in a relationship I don't like to play those kinds of games.

Now a lot of you people reading this book will be thinking, "But Bobby, that shouldn't have been a problem. You guys were doing movies and fucking all these other guys on-camera. What's the difference?"

Well, for me the difference was that that was work, and I left what I did at work, and that was Bobby Blake, and I left him at work. When I was doing porn I was never in love with any of the people I had sex with. I never made love to anyone on-screen; I was never even affectionate with them. You can't make love with somebody you're not in love with—there are none of those inner feelings to express. So that to me was a totally different thing; it was the job and nothing more.

My belief was that when we left the shoot we became who we were born to be. I believe in the family unit in a relationship. I believe in working hard to make your house a home. I believe that there should be rules and regulations in any house where there's more than one person living in it. I believe if you step over the line and transgress the rules one after the other, then gradually you turn the home back into a house and create an emotionally devastating atmosphere.

I expressed all this to Flex, and he seemed to understand. But subsequent to that conversation I several times caught him in bed with other guys, which was hurtful to me.

Sometime into the second year of our relationship I was contacted by an agent who said there was a guy in Paris who wanted to meet me and was willing to pay ten thousand dollars for the privilege. Flex at that point was somewhat jealous of me going off and having sex for money and didn't want me to do it. My attitude was that money is money. But I didn't want to hurt his feelings. I talked the situation over with some of my closest friends—Jermaine my ex, and Dee, my old friend from Memphis—and they both said I should take the money and go to Paris.

Still I felt awkward about it. I spoke to the agent and he said he would be willing to fly Flex over to Paris, too; that that was how keen this client was to meet me. And after all Flex was a handsome black bodybuilder, too; it wasn't as if I was proposing to drag some unattractive, out-of-condition loser along with me.

This client was a bodybuilder himself; he had a great physique, a gorgeous body, and that was part of why I was willing to take the job.

So I made all these arrangements to accommodate Flex. Then after all that it turned out that he couldn't go anyway; he couldn't get a passport because he owed child support. And you know what? I was so much in love with him that I cancelled Paris and stayed home with him.

What happened then was that the guy actually flew over to Florida to meet me. As I wasn't travelling I only charged him five thousand dollars, which was a loss of money for me. But the lesson I learned from that experience was that Flex wanted to have fun with other folks for free, and I wasn't supposed to be jealous of that, but then he didn't want me to go and make a business deal that would pay the rent and put bread on the table—which was the sort of thing that I meant when I said earlier that I found him to have a somewhat contradictory attitude to what he was doing when it came to sex and business.

Later on he wanted to travel to see clients in Seattle, and it never seemed to occur to him that that was hypocrisy on his part.

At the same time as all that was going on, Flex was making films, some with me, some without. I believe he still makes films to this day, and escorts. Though he never commanded the fees I did he earned a fair bit of money from the adult movie business. He built up his profile and his image regularly appeared on box-covers—though often alongside mine. And in the end I do believe that that was part of what limited him; he never really established a persona independent of mine. When you watch his performances on film, especially next to mine, it seems to me they lack conviction. It's like he's trying to do what I do rather than establish himself on his own terms.

I guess the truth is that he took on my name but he wasn't the person who built the franchise behind that name, and so the respect still flowed back to me. At events fans would come up to him and say, "You're Bobby Blake's lover, right?" Instead of acknowledging him as "Flex-Deon Blake, the porn star." That upset him a lot, and he always told me when it happened. And all I could really do was advise him to do something on his own and stop imitating what I was doing.

I had never imitated anyone. But I was a hard act to follow.

We did have good times though, me and Flex. Good

times and wild times.

One time we had been booked to do a show in Atlanta, at a club called The Warehouse. This would have been during Pride weekend. There were thousands of people in that club. It was on two, maybe three levels. Anyway, we were up there on a raised platform and I was into it and Flex was into it *[handwritten: Again no regard for my part Mr.]* and I turned him sideways on to the audience and I began to penetrate him on stage. I shoved my dick up him right there in front of everyone. I started to fuck him hard and it drove the crowd crazy—them Goddamn people rushed the stage! Security had to get us off. It was like they went wild because they hadn't seen nothing like that before at that club. Unbelievable. So that was fun in a scary kind of way.

Another time we had a very different kind of experience. We were special guests on a cruise, a week-long cruise to the U. S. islands, Puerto Rico, the Bahamas, St. Claire, St. Thomas, I don't remember all of them. It was a gay cruise and it was very nice, very relaxing. We didn't have to do much; just some autograph signings and hosting a costume party. They had a talent show on the ship where Flex sang— he has a good gospel-type voice—and I read some poetry I had written.

I also had a chance to talk to the crew, and they would say things like, "Wow, I didn't know you could talk like that." Or, "I didn't know you had that much sense. I didn't know you were that intelligent."

"Damn," I would reply. "Do you really think porn stars are the most uneducated, unintelligent people?"

And actually yes, people do have that perception, and part of the reason for writing this book is to show how wrong that perception is. There are a lot of people who have done porn and enjoyed doing it—lawyers, police officers, people in great professions, people wanting to put themselves through school—who are in no way stupid. And of those of us who have left the business, J. C. Carter is doing a law degree, I'm doing a law degree, and I believe Flex is now doing a business studies degree.

I've been asked about my poetry. It was about black gay men and the experiences of being a black gay man, and went in deep, and was well-received when I performed it on the cruise. It's locked away now in a storage facility, along with all my fan mail, poems people have sent me, and paintings and pictures fans have done of me.

Something was going deeply wrong. I found myself at a point in my life where from the outside everything looked like it was going great. My career as a porn star was on the rise. I was getting more and more work and commanding higher and higher fees. I had a handsome, sexy partner who was in the business and so understood that side of me, and with whom I was very much in love. Blatino was taking off and money was rolling in from that. As a performer and celebrity I was in demand, and I was meeting mainstream stars in the worlds of sport and entertainment and being lit up by their fame and wealth. From the outside it looked perfect. Yet inside was another story.

I call it the Marilyn Monroe syndrome. She was looked on as pretty much the most beautiful woman in the world. She was a powerful celebrity who looked like she had everything going for her, but on the inside she was miserable. Yet there she was before the public, always with a smile on her face. And that's how I felt during the second year I was with Flex; I would travel with him, and smile, and hide what was going on on the inside.

See, I was very much in love with Flex. I loved him in a consuming way, in a moth-battering-against-a-lightbulb way. And my love for him, and his response to that love, ended up driving me literally out of my mind.

CHAPTER TWENTY-SIX:

DESCENT INTO THE MAELSTROM

Descent into the Maelstrom is a story by Edgar Allan Poe which describes the battle by a ship's crew to avoid being sucked down by a monster whirlpool. During the second and third years I was with Flex, it described my mental state as well.

It's always hard to explain after the event why things stack up in a way that becomes unbearable.

One big background element was that my career, in which Flex was so involved, was so damn exhausting.

Making the films was the easy part; it only took a couple of hours. The promotion of them, the hosting of parties, the relentless networking, and the sideline of escort work, were all much more draining. I was pouring a lot of energy into promoting my persona and as a result I was neglecting my inner self. This would have been tiring enough, but I was also

His pursuit of money over people.

pouring massive amounts of energy into promoting Flex's persona, and into supporting him in our private lives as my mate.

All that time I was hearing warning signs that I ignored.

Actually, they were there right from the very beginning.

The first time I visited Flex down in Florida he took me to a soul food restaurant called Louie's, one of a chain. There were two black queens in there eating a meal at a nearby table. They recognized me and came over and introduced themselves to us, all excited to meet a real-life porn star. They were in the funeral home business, I recall. Anyway, they talked to us, and I told them that me and Flex was lovers. At that point Flex went to the restroom. The guys followed him with their eyes as he went. The moment he had gone one of them turned and said to me in a confidential tone, "You don't have nothing there but a ho."

"What you mean?" I asked, an edge to my tone.

"Hell, he been with everybody in the whole state of Florida!"

Well, Flex being so good-looking I assumed the guy was jealous of him for managing to get with me. Jealous and bad-mannered. So I brushed it off.

But I came to find out by and by that Flex did have a reputation down there for casual promiscuity. I mean, everyone has a past, but *damn!* It ended up seeming like he had slept with the whole of South Florida. If he had never gotten into the porn business he would still have had more sex than most people do who get into it.

As was usual with me I put my emotions aside and looked

at it in a businesslike way—if I've already slept with half the city of Memphis and then I do some movies, why would any of those guys buy them? They've already had the real thing for free. But on a more personal level of course it was hurtful to me to have total strangers tell me right to my face that my mate was a ho.

[handwritten: This is an addiction like all others. Can be reconfigured. Wasn't prepared to help or be judgmental.]

Another warning sign came from those around me. I was always generous with Flex, and as I've said before, particularly when we'd been apart for whatever reason, I would always give him a gift bag, not necessarily a lavish one, but to show him I loved him and was thinking of him, and I arranged birthday parties for him. But while I was doing all this my friends were coming to me and saying, "You know something? He's not very appreciative of what you do."

At first I didn't want to hear it, but I respected my friends and I knew they cared for me. I started to pay attention and I had to conclude they were right.

[handwritten: This is what friends are for.]
[handwritten: Astounded that he did generate such loyalty based on the character he reveals.]

One time I found out that Flex was cheating on me in a particularly hurtful way. We had set up email addresses that were very similar to each other's, *Bodysogreat* and *Bodysogood*, and sometimes people would message me mistaking me for Flex. If I had a mind to I might play along with them to see what they had to say.

This particular incident I'm talking about happened the week after Flex's birthday weekend. Now, as well as throwing a party for Flex to celebrate his actual birthday, I took him for a meal at a steakhouse a day or two before. We had a nice time, and afterwards he had a family obligation he had to go to and I didn't think anything more about it. Well.

"I really enjoyed watching my lover fuck you till you cried."

That was the message that appeared on my computer screen. I felt as if I had been punched in the gut. But what was I going to do about it? I could have replied pretending to be Flex. I was tempted to, but I didn't. Instead I chose to be direct and replied, "This isn't Flex, this is Bobby, his lover."

A long wait.

"Oh," came the eventual answer. "Sorry, man."

"When was this?"

"Last Thursday evening."

"We was out for a meal last Thursday," I typed. "You lying."

"Flex got a phone call."

I remembered that he did.

"And he told you he had to go see his sister, it was a family emergency."

"Yeah."

"He didn't even hardly finish his meal."

"So—"

"So he came to see me. And my lover fucked him in front of me."

This happened to me several times. Flex said he had gone to the gym and it turned out he had been off fucking with some guy, Flex said this and that. Now when it comes down to it you have to deal with reality; you have to face things as they are, and I did. But it was extremely painful for me.

Flex was adventurous; he had a lot of things inside him

[handwritten marginal note:] Puzzled by this why on earth get this into which will only pain him more. Already knows from what was said that occurred. Even more disgusting is the content on the other email which will be too crappy to sell out there. No sense of common decency that you know the pain it will cause just ensure that it's given under the guise of candour.

that had to come out, not just sexually but overall. But sex was a huge factor for him. I came to find that most of his so-called friends were men he'd slept with before they became friends, and this impacted negatively on our relationship.

His fascination with sex was massively magnified by his involvement in the porn industry. Porn brought him attention, and he was like a kid in a candy store, unable to say no. It was the opposite mentality to mine: I had always had all the attention I needed long before I went into adult films. So while I understood his mindset, I didn't share it, and that, too, was harmful to our relationship.

I also came to suspect that Flex was doing drugs. One time we went to the house of a friend of his and while we were there this friend offered him a joint. Flex turned it down, but I asked myself, why would his friend offer him a joint in front of me? Why would he feel comfortable doing that? When we got home I asked Flex about it, and he just dusted it off and shrugged and said, "I don't know why he did that."

Another time we had a booking at a club called The Warehouse, which is in New York. We were in the dressing room getting ready to put on a show when another of his friends came in twiddling this rolled-up dollar bill between his fingers in an attention-getting kind of way. I can be a bit naïve sometimes, and I recall looking at this guy and wondering why in fuck he was rolling a dollar bill like that. Flex glanced at me and said, "No, I don't want any." At which point the penny dropped for me: cocaine.

The guy left, and I confronted Flex about it. I said,

"Look, this stuff is not adding up. You are doing drugs. These people are not going to be so comfortable to offer you that in front of me unless they know you're into it. This is the second time this has happened right before my eyes."

But he denied it, and because I loved him, I let it slide. I closed my eyes. *The danger of love being willfully blind*

The fact I was being the financially responsible half of our relationship certainly didn't help things. When I added it up I found that I was covering 95% of our outgoings. I was even paying his truck note. Flex is not a bill-payer. As you'll recall he couldn't come to Paris with me because he owed child support, and I do believe that you have an absolute duty to support the children you father. Flex didn't, and after we broke up he ended up being kicked out of the apartment we had leased together for not paying the rent. All the stuff I had left him in the apartment, he lost all of that. His truck got repossessed. All those lessons I had tried to teach him about responsibility and business-mindedness came to nothing, and for a time he actually had to leave Florida.

Flex and I still talk. I still love him, but for so long he went along in life pretending and pretending and blaming other people that it was painful for me to speak with him. For instance, after he and I broke up he was in another relationship, with a guy named Karl Stokes, who sadly passed away earlier this year of a heart attack. They were together for over three years.

Flex would call me up and say that he and Karl hadn't been talking in a while, that Karl was mad with him.

"I don't know why," Flex said. "I've been filling out job

applications like crazy, I've put out about twenty of them."

In other words Flex wasn't working, and Karl had got tired of taking care of his lazy ass.

"You're doing the same shit you've been doing all of your life," I lectured him. "You blame it on your wife. You say she won't let you keep the kids but you don't support them. You bitch about how your ex-lovers never did nothing for you, how they left you in a hole, but you never paid your way; that's the hole you ended up in. When you blame everyone else then face it, the problem is *you*. Something's wrong with *you*. You moan about your relationship with Karl but you're not supporting him. It's the same bullshit you fed me when you and me was going out."

He had to admit I was right, just as he'd had to admit I was right when I told him that a lot of the people he thought of as friends were only fair-weather, and wouldn't be around when the hurricanes hit.

I heard that after Karl died Flex was out on his ass and had to go stay with his sister back in Florida. Then he got a place he's sharing with a room-mate. He's nearly fifty and that's his situation—he has no substance, no assets as far as I know, and, according to his own website, he still escorts. So I don't know. He runs a group called BrothasNDaSpirit for black gay Christians coming to terms with their sexuality, so I guess he's doing what he's doing.

Currently I'm not in a relationship. I've been single for five and a half years. I've dated guys, but I've never involved anyone as fully in my life as I did Flex. And you can believe me when I say at the first sign of trouble—alcohol or drug abuse, lying—boom! It's over. I have zero tolerance. I don't need anybody in my life to make me happy; I'm extremely happy as I am.

But in the meantime Flex was burning me out. It began to affect me mentally. The lesson I eventually learned from what I went through with him was that the pain he caused me didn't mean he was a bad person; it just meant that I wasn't for him and he wasn't for me. But that's something you can only see later, when you get some distance from a situation.

I guess I made the age-old mistake of thinking I could change him; I thought I could make him want what he didn't want, and not want what he did want, and that's as good a way of torturing yourself as any I can think of. The lesson of life is—what you see is what you gon' get, and if you blind yourself to the truth of that, then it's your own fault for staying in the situation.

Unfortunately for me I was blinded by love.

My mind started to unravel. I would call up Dee and Jermaine and complain endlessly about the problems I was having in my relationship. They were both always there for me, and in that I was blessed, but I must have worn them down somewhat.

"Big brother," Dee would tell me over and over, "you've got to be strong." He didn't know what else to say.

"You don't love yourself," Jermaine told me bluntly one day. It was hard for me to hear that from him. I just felt he was meddling.

"You're just jealous," I told him.

"I'm not jealous," he said. "I love you. And you're focusing more on your partner's needs than on your own. You're ignoring yourself, and it's dragging you down. Spend time with yourself. Go and eat out, eat dinner by yourself. Go to a movie by yourself."

I knew Jermaine was right, and I did all those things, but they weren't enough. I even managed to persuade Flex to go to couples counseling with me, and the counselor repeated what my friends were saying; he told Flex that he was selfish, and he told me that I needed to develop a life aside from him. But Flex wouldn't pull back from doing his own thing, and I was so deeply in love with Flex I just couldn't let go. I couldn't pull back from the maelstrom.

Around that time I caught Flex in bed with yet another guy, and it would have been after that that I became overwhelmed and started to really come apart at the seams. I felt I was a good person. I was trying to make my relationship work. Why was it all going so wrong? I went to a Catholic bishop I knew in Florida and cried on his shoulder.

"You need to get yourself together and work this out," he said, and he prayed for me. But I was at a point where I couldn't get myself together. I was slipping and couldn't get a grip, and nobody's prayers would help me. I hit rock bottom.

One endless dreary night I felt that I couldn't cope any more. I didn't feel suicidal. I'd been through too much in my life for that; time had tried me and I had endured. But life felt unbearably painful and I could see no solutions. Medication couldn't take the pain away; no doctor, no pharmacist could take it from me. Words sounded good but they had no healing in them. I had no friends in Florida; all my friends were back in Memphis, or Los Angeles. And they had given me all the advice they had to give, and I couldn't bear to hear it again because I couldn't act on it. I was horribly isolated. I had been attending Flex's church but I didn't properly participate because everything in me was focused on him and my futile need to make our house a home, so I couldn't call on the pastor for advice or support. I felt as if I had turned my back on both my life and my God. I was alone, it was late, there were no counselors I could call. My pain was like a cancer eating away at me. I needed someone professional to talk to. Someone uninvolved, who hadn't heard it all before.

Nearby there was a psychiatric hospital. Hands trembling on the wheel I drove over there and mercifully there was a counselor available for me to speak with. He listened and he told me what everyone else had told me; that I needed to put the focus back on myself. Simple words, but somehow this time they helped.

Afterwards I thought how Flex had driven me to this; he had driven me to a mental hospital. And I thought of my mother and the pain in her life. I can't say exactly why, but that was a turning point for me. I realized that however many prayers were said for me, or whatever the doctors or counselors said to me, it was down to me to transform my situation. That it was only when I got sick and tired of being sick and tired that I could draw the line and say enough was enough.

I found myself singing the old song, "Father, I stretch my hand to thee." It was a song I had sung many times before, but now I meant the words with all my heart. I cried unto Him. I stretched out my hand and at that moment God began to deal with me. He gave me an inner peace that friends and counselors could not give me. And He enabled me to find the strength to do what needed to be done and put things behind me.

I ended my relationship with Flex. It took me a few weeks to get to the point, but then I just woke up one morning and wham! That was it, decision made. He begged me to stay but I said no. I let him have the apartment and pretty much everything in it because I didn't want any conflict or argument. God had instructed me: "I know you paid for this stuff, but he'll just use arguing over it as a way of keeping you there." So I let him have it all. Not, as you've already seen, that he profited by it.

Leaving that apartment for the final time, stripped all but naked as it were, I felt as though I had passed some sort of test; God had tested me, and I had let Him guide my heart, and I had weathered the storm through obedience to His will. I believe He gave me the strength I needed because He could see that I was a good man. And I believe that I became a better and wiser person through the suffering I endured in that relationship.

And so I returned home, to Memphis.

CHAPTER TWENTY-SEVEN:

ESCORTING

Escorting was something I only did for a brief period of time. I did it with both men and women. I don't really like to use the word 'escorting' because that suggests something different from the reality of what was actually happening. And what was actually happening was—I had become extremely well-known in a very short space of time. I was a celebrity. People get fascinated with celebrities. I was a celebrity in the world of sex, so people generally had a sexual response towards me. They knew I got paid to fuck on film and so they expected to pay me for my time and attention. They offered me money and I was willing to take their money. *Reality of eem differentials which will never cease.*

The more sexual a situation was, the more I was all about business. By this time my persona was pretty much established as an extremely aggressive top who crossed over into leather and S/M and violent abuse. I would often team up with guys to act out scenarios because it was more fun than doing it on your own. We had clients—one was the CEO of a big shipping company in the United States—and they liked you to beat the shit out of them. They'd pay you big money to come to the door of their house—and usually they'd be living in some big old mansion—and they'd want you to come in their houses and knock hell out of 'em. They'd even want you to take a baseball bat and beat them all around the house. Well, I loved that. It was fun and it came easy to me. I'd beat their ass so fucking hard they probably regretted it. But then they'd come back for more so I guess they loved it too. And I got paid.

One time—this would have been after I broke up with Flex, when I was in the tail-end of escorting—I was dating this guy who was a doctor, working in the State Department of Education. We were in New York vacationing and we ended up in this guy's apartment one evening, and the guy offered us two thousand dollars apiece to shit on him. Just that.

"Damn," I said. "For that money I'll shit on you." So I did. I shit on him.

"Hell, no," my date said. I gave him a look. "I can't do it, man," he said.

"Hell, yeah, you can," I said. "Just do it, then we can go."

"I can't do this," he repeated.

"You better," I said. "Two two-thousand dollar shits in one minute!"

Well, my date got over his inhibitions, and we got our money. End of story.

Now I don't understand what that guy got out of being

People have all sorts of fetishes at least they arn't marrethim — but how is one able to shit on demand?

shit on. That's the only thing I don't understand. But it was business, and I did it.

In such situations I always took steps to protect myself from foolishness. For example: I met this guy off my website. This is while I was still in L. A. We talked and he wanted to meet. I told him okay, but that I didn't tolerate people doing drugs around me. He said fine, but I had a feeling he was doing something. His name was 'Ron'. He wanted me to go with him to New York for a week. I charged him twelve thousand dollars. I made him pay a deposit up front and I got a round-trip ticket.

Well, we get on the plane and the minute we're in the air the motherfucker starts acting silly—laughing, grinning, babbling on about nothing. I said to myself, "Damn, this motherfucker's on drugs." I was mad.

We got to New York and I paid him no attention. He got mad with me and went in one of those books and hired another escort to come over. My response? Fine. I got the rest of the money from his ass and left. I'm always prepared for the worst.

And I always get paid. One time me and Flex, we had gone out of town. We were in St. Louis and this guy wanted us to be guests at a private party he was hosting. We told him up front what the deal was, how much we would charge, and he agreed. He was charging guests on the door so must have made himself a few grand on the deal.

Anyway, at the end of the party, when it was time, we asked for the money. I said, "You ready to pay us, right?"

"Yeah," he says. And the motherfucker goes and takes his clothes off, comes back in a robe with a bottle of lube.

"What the fuck you doin'?" I ask.

"I'm gon' give you all some ass," he said.

"No, you ain't, motherfucker," I said. "We want our money."

"Oh," he says, blinking kind of stupidly, "I didn't come up with all the money."

"Huh?" I said. "With all those Goddamn people? Motherfucker, I tell you what—"

I went through that guy's house. I took all his jewelry. His TV. His VCR. Everything. I must have taken about half a million dollars' worth of shit out of his house.

"You got till three o'clock tomorrow afternoon to have my money," I told him. "If you don't, this shit is going back to Florida with me. You can call the police if you want to. See what happens."

Well, he didn't call the police, and the next day he came up with the money.

When it came to money, I wasn't playing. I remember doing a show in a club in Miami. The guy who ran the club was named 'Terry' and used to work for a funeral home. Now, I had a high booking fee, but I always made it clear up front that that was what I charged. So I turned up and did a show, and when it came time to get paid he only had half the money we had agreed on.

"You gon' pay me," I told him. He had a pile of gold round his neck. I took it off him. "There's always collateral," I said. "In your house. Round your neck. On your hands." I took his jewels. "If you want a fight we can go there," I told him. He cried like a bitch.

I guess he was used to dealing with guys he could wave off, who would say, "Okay, I'll come back later."

"Not me," I said. "You'll be coming looking for me if you want your jewels." And he did.

Sometimes it was fun, though. When I was in London I met a guy, an American guy who turned out to be the vice-president of American Express there. I met him while I was working out at the big gay gym in Soho.

By the by, one thing that surprised me about London was seeing so many white boys with big dicks and nice asses. In the United States it's like the white boys got little dicks, but these boys' dicks had got as big as ours, ten and eleven inches. I told this one guy, "You got some black in you!"

"What do you mean?" he said.

"Look at your dick," I said. "It's bigger than mine!"

"Oh, it's like that all over here," he said.

And I thought, "Damn!"

Anyway, I met this vice-president and we dated for a while. He had a penthouse in New York right next door to Whoopi Goldberg's penthouse. He had paintings on the walls worth two or three hundred thousand dollars and a huge dining table we would sit at to eat.

"Table big enough for King Arthur and all the knights and there ain't nothing but you and me," I told him. "And all these Goddamn paintings! I could take all these paintings to the pawn shop!"

I made him laugh, and he was good to me. I didn't want

Nothg more than prostitution no matter how he frames it

for anything while I was seeing him, and that was fine by me. That was an example of a more complicated situation— he was paying for everything and he was paying for me, but in a more relationship-romance-oriented situation. So I was being paid for, but it wasn't exactly escorting, and it certainly wasn't being paid to perform any particular sex act.

It was almost never just about sex anyway. Sometimes it was more of a status thing, guys would want me to be in their presence in a public setting. They would want to hang out with me and be seen with me, and experience what it meant to be out with Bobby Blake the Porn Star. A sort of showing off, I guess. Other times a guy would want something more private and intimate: dinner, a movie, quiet times in his home. Someone to talk to. Someone big and masculine who would listen to his troubles, and who I guess symbolized a sort of safety and protection—strong arms around you. And who would demand nothing but money in return.

With either of those types of people sex might or might not be involved. Whether it was involved or not, they were paying for my presence more than they were paying to have sex with me. My attitude was always, hey, if they've got more money than they need and they want to share it with me, don't knock it!

Sometimes I would be offered things in a wholly non-sexual way. Another guy I got to know in New York once bought me a truck; $27,000 it cost him. He came to see me, put it on his credit card and handed me the keys. No strings, no obligations. Just a gift. In any case, you know me well enough by now to know that no one was going to buy me with gifts. Even today that guy will buy me stuff; he'll send me money if I ask for it.

Perhaps the oddest thing I did relating to escorting was to be the prize in a competition in *Black Inches* magazine. The competition was to "Win a Date with Bobby Blake." Readers would write in asking for a date, and enclosing photos of themselves. I would pick a winner, we would go on a date and be photographed at dinner or at a club, wherever the winning guy wanted to go, and the photographs would appear in the next issue of *Black Inches*. It was odd because the setup was romantic—dinner and a date—but the people writing in knew me as this aggressive porn star. *Truly pathetic*

Well, thousands of guys wrote in, some of them extreme- *but so* ly cute, so it was easy to pick someone I'd be happy to go out *many* with for the evening. It was also a reminder of how well- *people* known I had become. Most of the letters were flattering and *lonely &* charming, but there were also some crazy ones, reminders of *in need* how fame has its price. I'll talk about them in a later chap- *validation* ter: Stalkers. Because I've had a few.

Black Inches was always very supportive of me. They reviewed every film I made, did photo-shoots, interviewed me, and gave me my own column. The first time I went to New York was through doing a cover for them. The flight I hated—flying west coast to east coast is my least favorite journey of all time—but the signing, at a really famous New York club called L'Esqualita, was a great success. I've always had a huge fan base on the East Coast.

One guy I signed for, we got talking and he really liked

me. We exchanged numbers and spoke, then met, again. We connected and started to see each other. At which point I discovered he was the head of one of the New York gangs!

I was amazed because even though of course I knew gay people are in every walk of life I still hadn't expected a gang boss to be gay. I dated him for a time, and his gang members were like bodyguards to me. I didn't want for anything, but as so often those who give you so much materially prove to be too possessive, and I quickly drew back from the situation.

As an escort I had a good many celebrity clients. Again, it wasn't always about sex—sometimes I would go to a guy's home and he would cry on my shoulder and I knew it was because his relationship had gone bad. I could see from the state of the room that his mate was gone, that they'd been arguing, and he just wanted someone to talk to. And I would listen, and offer comfort. And then I would go.

One time I was at the Atlanta airport. Atlanta being one of the black gay capitals of the world they have a lot of black gay men working at the airport, and they were coming up to me and asking for autographs. And while I was signing pictures a celebrity came by with his entourage. I can't name names, but it was this gorgeous boy, a singer I used to have a crush on big-time. And he asks one of the guys I'm signing for, "Who is he?"

"He's a film star."

"I've never seen him in no movie."

"Well. . . ." the guy I'd just signed for tailed off and shrugged.

The singer turns to me. "I've never seen you in no movie," he says.

"Well, my name's Bobby," I say.

"I've never seen you in no movie," he says. "But I want me a picture."

They was all nude pictures, so I said to him, "I promise you you don't want no picture."

Well, he looked down at the sheaf of pictures I was holding in my hand and he didn't change his bearing one bit.

"Just give me a picture like I axed," he said. So I did. I signed it, and I gave it to him, and then his flight was called and he and his entourage went on their way.

I've been invited to celebrity parties and been amazed to find who's lovers with whom. I've been able to walk on the inside and see so many things, and I can tell you, Hollywood is full of surprises.

My celebrity clients included football players, basketball players, and movie stars. I've been flown first-class all over the world. I've entertained politicians from Washington D.C.; I've been with government officials from all over the world. I've slept with them and sometimes their girlfriends, too. I've slept with fine masculine men, black, white, latino, who you would never guess were gay. I've had the TV on and seen men I've dealt with, stars who've gotten divorced time and again, and wondered if the wives are going to finally speak up and say, "We broke up because he's gay." But I guess they get paid off because they never do.

Sometimes I look back to my childhood days and think how strange it is that this little nappy-headed boy, who first of all was told he was going to die, grew up into this man with this unique physique, this man who's seen as so desirable that the rich and famous will pay to fly him all over the world just to be with him. *This is what I don't understand*

A lot of books people kiss and tell on who they slept with, but I'm not that type of person. These guys entrusted me to withhold their identities, and I'm not one to cash in on someone else's name.

I would say that for all their wealth and fame I often found their lives to be sad. They had married a girl to create a smokescreen, to conceal their true sexuality, and so of course the marriage would fail. And I would say to these guys, "Dude, just go head on and be who you are. Let these women alone because you're getting divorced time after time." I guess you could call it a Hollywood cycle.

So I was dealing with these guys and they were leading these glittering, dishonest lives, and it was fascinating but depressing. And despite the access my desirability as a sex partner had bought me, my position in relation to those lives was a totally unreal one.

I was at this movie star's house one time, a very popular guy, and I was like, "Wow," because he had all these manservants and maidservants at his beck and call and wanted for nothing, and he was gracious towards me and made me very welcome. His home was so opulent it was like being in a dream, and I enjoyed being there. But afterwards, when I got home, I realized what should have been obvious to me all along—that all that stuff was his stuff, not mine. It was his life, and I was only borrowing it for an hour or two. I needed to focus on my own life, not someone else's. I needed to wake up, not drift along in a dream.

It would have been different if it had been a date and he had been trying to get to know me. But he had been hiring Bobby Blake the Porn Star. I had been playing a part and providing him with a fantasy; the real me hadn't been there at all.

And so I quit escorting.

CHAPTER TWENTY-EIGHT:

FANS

Most of the time I'm real grateful for my fans. I'm proud to have given so many people pleasure with my work. It's gratifying to be recognized and appreciated for what I've done in the field of adult entertainment, and I'm privileged to have had the chance to become well known enough to be able to raise people's awareness of issues around HIV-AIDS as well.

Although some of my fans are rich, and they've flown me all over the world, from Berlin to South Africa and beyond, most of my fans are ordinary folks, and I'm deeply touched by their recognition and enthusiasm for what I've done.

Oftentimes it's fun to be recognized, to be asked for autographs, to be bumped up to first class because the steward knows my films, to be sat at the best table in the restaurant because the maitre d' is a Bobby Blake fan. Sometimes it can be a little strange, as when guys come up to me with their girlfriends by their sides and say, "Man, I know you."

"Yeah? You sure you know me?"

"I'm sure, man. I know you from somewhere."

"Maybe a basketball game," I suggest.

"No, no, that weren't it." The guy can't quite remember where he recognizes me from.

"Ask me one more time," I'll tell him, casting an eye at his girlfriend, "and I'm gon' tell you!"

Other times it'll be a guy with his girlfriend and they'll be quite upfront—they've seen my movies and want me to do a threesome with them.

I remember here in Memphis at the time of the Lennox Lewis/Mike Tyson fight. I was down on Beale Street, which is a real popular street full of bars and restaurants, and I had on a tank-top. And this guy came up to me and said, "Damn, you bigger than the boxers! Damn, you got big arms."

Right away I knew he wanted a threeway, because why else would he be saying that in front of his girlfriend? And he was good-looking, and she was good-looking, so I was happy to oblige. I fucked both of 'em that night.

Another time I was eating in some restaurant in South Beach and a man came up to me and introduced himself to me, and the lady he was with as his wife.

"We really enjoy your movies," he said.

I'm like, "Huh? But that's your wife standing right next to you."

"I like your movies too," she said.

That kind of thing happened to me surprisingly often. I've come to find a lot of women like to put on a strap-on and fuck their husbands. Being in the porn business means people think you can't be shocked, and they'll often want to tell you every little thing they get up to. But sometimes I am amazed—at heart I'm still this little country boy.

Fans sometimes come up to me and say, "You brought a new era to the porn industry. You brought masculinity. We like the rugged style you have. We like the verbal, the way you talk. You brought something to the porn industry, something that's never been done before." And that pleases me, because that's what I hoped to do in my performances on film.

It can all get a little much, though. You have to remember that the word "fan" was originally short for "fanatic."

I was once a special guest at a small club in Kansas City, Missouri. I was booked there to dance but when I arrived it was so rammed I could hardly get in through the door. I had to have four security guards around me just to get through the crowd to the dressing room.

There wasn't any space for me to dance, but I came out the dressing room, took off my clothes, and them Goddamn people, they pushed the guards out the way and shoved forward and before I knew it I ended up on the floor. At that point it was all so out of control I began to be in fear of my life, lying there oily and naked, getting trampled by the mob.

With all the strength in my body I forced my way back up onto my feet and just pushed people away from me, and somehow managed to get back into the dressing room. It was one of the scariest experiences of my life, and the result of bad organization on the part of the people running the club. Bad organization and greed in allowing too many people in. I've put the club's name out of my mind and wasn't surprised to hear that it closed down a little while later.

At least I made sure I got paid.

In that instance the problem was bad organization—my fans were just over-enthusiastic, and that's understandable. But sometimes you get people coming up to you who are genuinely crazy, and that's really disturbing. It was Edward James who said to me, when we were over in Berlin for the Hustler's Ball, "Bobby, you built a world-wide reputation for yourself. Some people take all this very seriously, and you have to understand that. We know who you really are, and how you really feel, but they don't understand that. They want the dream," he told me. "They want the fantasy."

The most recent case of that happening to me was a few years back when I was in Atlanta, Georgia. I was outside a club called Tracks, just hanging out and doing my own thing. It was a Pride weekend and there were thousands and thousands of people around. I do have a huge fan-base, and plenty of people would come up and say hello to me or want to shake hands or what have you. On the whole the easy, masculine way I carry myself helps stop trouble from starting.

Anyway, I was there with my play-sons—who are both guys in their twenties—just talking and enjoying the scene, when this guy grabbed me from behind. He put both his

arms round me, pinning my arms to my sides, and started in
with, "Ooh, Bobby Blake, Bobby Blake! I've got to have you,
Bobby Blake!"

Well at first I was just embarrassed because he was going
a little far in his enthusiasm. And I was saying to myself,
well, he's just playing. It's nothing serious, humor him, so I
laughed.

"I've got to have you," he said again, and then his voice
kind of changed. "If I can't have you," he said, "nobody will."

Well, I still thought he was playing, but enough was
enough. "Okay," I said. "You can let me go now."

But he didn't let me go. And because he had grabbed me
from behind I hadn't had a chance to see his face, and he had
my arms pinned to my sides.

"You let me go," I repeated, more assertively this time.
But he wouldn't let me go; he just got louder and louder and
suddenly I realized, this motherfucker's crazy, he's for real. At
that point my play-sons realized the guy was crazy too, and
they pulled him off me.

Afterwards we came to find he had a knife in his pocket.

Another creepy thing happened to me when I was doing
a special guest appearance at Club Metro in Atlanta, dancing. Club Metro was on Cypher Street back then. This was
early on in my porn career, and in my early days I made a
point of not staying at the guest hotel whoever booked me
would offer to arrange. Instead I would book myself into
cheap hotels, both to save money and so no one would know
where I was staying to bother me.

On this occasion I had booked myself into a Red Roof

Inn on North Druid Hill and Buford Highway. I got back to the hotel after the gig and went to my room. The telephone rang.

"You're Bobby Blake," a voice said. "I've got your room number. I know where you're at. You just left Club Metro, and you're going to be with me or you're not going to be with anybody. I know the car you're driving."

Well, that particular incident didn't make me frightened, it made me mad. But it combined with the later incident in Georgia to make me consider the issue of my personal safety more seriously.

Another factor was talking with Pat, one of the editors at *Black Inches*, about some of the letters people would send me.

Over the years I've received thousands and thousands of fan letters, and of course most of them are flattering and enthusiastic and a pleasure to read. People send me poems they've written about me, and paintings they've done of me. One fan by the name of Dan Drew sent me three oil paintings he'd done of me, and I donated those pictures to a charity called The Haven, which is part of the HIV-AIDS charity Friends for Life, and they auctioned those pictures off to raise money for HIV-AIDS awareness. But some people took it all too far. It was like they would have me or no one would have me. They would include drawings of animals with their heads cut off, insane shit like that.

Now, I wasn't going to allow my life to become limited because a very few crazy people were out there, but I did start to take security seriously. Some people will have noticed I always tend to keep a crowd around me when I'm at any public event nowadays, and one or two of those people will always be bodyguards who are trained to deal with any threatening situations that arise.

Sometimes I need to get away from my fame. I love my gym in Memphis because most of the people who use it don't know who I am. I go early in the morning to get my work-out in, then I train a couple of people who don't know they're being trained by Bobby Blake the Porn Star. It's nice to get away from being known for a while.

But a lot of the time fame is fun, and having fans is fun. There are people who just adore me. They give me gifts, sometimes very valuable ones. They declare undying love and act crazy in ways that are harmless and even endearing. Sometimes I'll give them one of my cell-numbers so they can call me up and be amazed to find themselves having a real-life conversation with Bobby Blake the Porn-Star. I don't really understand it because I don't feel that way about any-one, and I know who I am.

Sometimes it feels unreal.

Sometimes my life is unbelievable.

CHAPTER TWENTY-NINE:

NIGGAS' REVENGE

(handwritten annotation): Why do they disrespect themselves by using this word now ... Was ... ed into a respectful term.

Niggas' Revenge was the last porn film I made. It was shot right at the start of 2001, so any supposedly new films of mine you see that are dated later than that have been spliced together using old footage from *Huge, Black, and Delicious* or *Big Black Bananas* or what have you. *Niggas' Revenge* was, no question, the most extreme film I made. It's also one of the most controversial adult films ever made, and that's how I wanted it to be—I had decided this was to be my last film, and I wanted to take it to the limit.

In it I also do one thing I went on to deeply regret.

Niggas' Revenge was a big seller at the time it was made, and still sells well today, but it's very much a specialist type of film, so I doubt a lot of my regular fans will have seen it. I can't do much better to express what it's about than quote what's written on the back of the box:

White neo-nazi supremacists [Bud, Dallas Chambers, and Chane Adams] *fuck with the wrong niggas and get their come-uppance from the huge-muscled, huge-cocked Blake Boys: Bobby, Flex-Deon, and Chris…and their Puerto-Rican buddy, Eric Top Stud. The nazis are arbitrarily and brutally used as fuck-holes, urinals, and cum repositories in the most controversial video of the decade.*

The director, Dick Wadd, was well-known for the extremity of his films, and he approached me to star in the film. He offered me a lot of money and I said yes.

There's no question that my persona and my performances got more violent as they went along, and no doubt that was why Dick Wadd thought of me for the film. My growing aggressiveness in my films was partly the product of my desire to find a way of taking each film I made that bit further. And partly I guess I was working my way to some sort of ultimate end-point for Bobby Blake the Porn Star. But as well as that I found it easy to be extremely sexually aggressive and I found it fun. I enjoyed not having to hold back. If I fucked you senseless, if I hit you, if I shoved your face in the concrete, made you suck my dick and lick my boots, if I spit in your face or pissed on you, I didn't hold back because I figured that you had either already seen some of my movies and knew what to expect, or the director had already warned you what I was about. You had chosen to take this position, you were up to date on it, so you were ready to take the punishment. I found not having to feel for you, not having to worry, liberating.

I never felt my aggressiveness went overboard. If anything I felt a need to be more aggressive, both physically and verbally, to blow the minds of the viewers, to supersede their expectations and even their understanding. As I became more extreme there were some people who wouldn't do movies with me. Particularly some women; they were scared I would really hurt them. That was down to a bi-sexual movie I made where I dragged the girl across the stage by her hair while calling her all kinds of bitches and made her suck my dick. The other females saw that, and they don't usually have that in their movies, so they thought, "Wow, that's too much for me," and they wouldn't work with me. But plenty of others would.

Around my second year in porn I started making some leather movies in addition to the regular ones. Usually it wasn't a big element. In Chi Chi LaRue's *In The Mix*, for instance, you'll notice that most of the black guys are wearing a certain amount of leather, but it's not a leather movie, it's not about dominance or submission or S/M. Similarly *Black, Sex & Leather* is a regular gang-bang type movie where the guys happen to be wearing leather. *Black Raven Gang-Bang* does have me in leather melting a black candle over a guy and fucking him with it, which is somewhat more of a fetish scenario. And *Black Warriors*, in which I star with Bam, has us in black leather and studs against a black backdrop fucking guys real aggressively over a specially-designed pommel-horse. That film did definitely have more of a sadistic tone to it, and I guess my leather films show the same progression from less rough to more rough in terms of the sex that you can detect in my regular films.

Leather itself wasn't something that ever particularly interested me or turned me on, though. In fact, sometimes it would even turn me off because some people in leather look like a mess. They think the leather will do all the work for them, whereas for me it only looks good on you if you look good in the first place. So, though I enjoy seeing leather on guys who take care of their bodies, I don't care about the leather in itself.

As I've said, *Niggas' Revenge* was my last movie, and Flex was one of my co-stars. Despite the difficulties in our relationship we went on making movies together until I quit the business. I'm told he's done a lot of films since *Niggas' Revenge* but that was the last one he performed in that I actually saw, and of course my main reason for watching it was that I was in it.

It was an expensive movie and is the most powerful movie of my career. In terms of performance I would say it sets the men apart from the boys. When you watch Flex and Chris Blake in that film you can tell the difference between the way I handled the other guys and they way they did. Flex and Chris just didn't have it in them to really dominate a situation in the way I did. In fact they were weak. Especially Chris. He was hired to be a top alongside me and Flex, but it was no surprise that he ended up in the pillory with me fucking his ass as well as the white guys' asses. That wasn't supposed to happen, the director hadn't planned it that way. But as in 97% of the movies I made I just took over and did what I wanted to do, and let what was inside of me come out.

I didn't hold back.

Afterwards one of the white models said to me, "Bobby, you enjoyed beating us."

And I said, "Yeah, I did."

We almost got busted by the cops on that film. That had happened to me once before, when we were filming the Paul Barresi prison movie *Iron Cage*. We were up in the mountains in a national park and I was fucking this white boy, this little white guy who had said something to make me mad, and I was fucking him so hard he was sliding down the mountain and hollering with each thrust of my dick deep into his ass. So I'm fucking him, he's yelling, the camera's turning and all of a sudden somebody shouts, "Damn! The rangers!"

Shit, I did a Superman on they ass! I got my clothes on so damn fast it was like I never had 'em off, and I was *gone*.

On *Niggas' Revenge,* what happened was we were shooting at the producer, Dick Wadd's home. The way the film was set up was me, Flex, and Chris, along with a shaven-headed black lady named Crystal Blake who was playing my wife, were supposedly moving into our new home in an upper-class white area. Despite it being upper-class our neighbors turn out to be a bunch of racist skinheads. Dick Wadd got them to improvise racist abuse to get us all riled up. Me, Flex, and Chris get mad and go out to deal with them. We get into a fight and end up shoving their faces in the dirt, pissing on them, and I beat one of them on the ass with a plank so hard the plank breaks across his butt.

Now that racist abuse did make me mad. I got so angry

that when I was beating those guys I was doing it for real. And evidently the neighbors must have seen or heard some of what was going on because they called the cops. I guess they thought I was beating someone half to death.

So the police showed up, wanting to know what the hell was going on. We kept out of sight and let Dick Wadd deal with it. Dick must have known the officers, because he told them, "Everything is okay, there isn't a problem here," and they accepted it and left. But it shows how real what we were doing was.

And I have to commend the guys playing the neo-nazis— Bud, Dallas Chalmers, and Chane Adams—because they took a genuine beating. It wasn't a fake movie; from the whipping with the belt to the breaking of the two-by-four over their asses, the slapping, the spitting, the making them drink piss, all of that was totally real.

At the time I wanted to do just one film that was totally extreme. I did it, and that was it. I was liberated from something. I had done what I needed to do. I retired from porn and went on with my life.

My one regret as far as *Niggas' Revenge* goes is that we made it without rubbers; there's a lot of unsafe fucking in that film. It was the only film I made in my entire career where I fucked without condoms. I'm very grateful that I'm HIV-negative despite that, but I do regret it because I think that if you're in the public eye you have a duty to be responsible and spread the message that safer sex is important. All the time I was making movies, and since my retirement from the adult entertainment industry, I've done a lot of work supporting HIV-AIDS awareness issues, so what did I think I was doing in that particular instance?

The only honest answer I can give is: we all make mistakes. And that was a mistake I made. I was caught up in an extreme mentality and an extreme situation and I didn't exercise proper control over myself. But what I would say to anybody, and in particular young people today, is don't let somebody else's mistake be your mistake. Don't use what I did as an excuse to do something you know isn't wise. Practice safer sex. You have the knowledge. Don't fool yourself that the new drugs are a magic bullet that's easy to take and has no consequence: HIV is still a very serious business. The latest figures tell us that the average extra length of life the retrovirals give to someone who becomes HIV+ is thirty-two point one years. The new drugs are a triumph of science, but if you get infected at age eighteen that still only takes you to fifty. I'm fifty and I still feel like I have my whole life before me!

With that one exception I was proud of *Niggas' Revenge*. I had taken Bobby Blake as far as he could go. I had achieved everything I had ever hoped of achieving in adult movies. I had fame and I had respect. I had money in the bank. I was determined to stop making films while I was on a high, and I did.

CHAPTER THIRTY:

THE PRODIGAL RETURNS

After *Niggas' Revenge* I retired from making adult films.

People say to me all the time, "Oh, you gon' come back, you gon' come back."

But I tell them, "No."

And I've been offered money I could probably use—just recently a studio in Miami offered me five thousand dollars just for a jerk-off scene—but I always turn it down. Because I'm not the kind of person who, once I've quit doing something, comes out of retirement to do it over again. Stop while you're at the top of your game is my philosophy. Do what you do and keep on moving forward in your life.

Something I don't think I've discussed so far is it's amazing how many guys who hit on me want to top me. I've asked them, "Why you want to do that so bad?"

"Well, we've seen how you do those guys in your movies," they say. "We want to do you that way." I guess their fantasy, their desire, is to turn the tables on me and prove themselves the ultimate men.

And I tell them, "It will never happen. And if it *was* going to happen, I'd do it in a movie where I'd get paid millions of dollars to do it."

But like I said, I'm retired. So I can say to all you guys out there fantasizing about topping Bobby Blake, or seeing me topped in a movie—it's not going to happen.

My relationship with Flex collapsed and I had no desire to remain in Florida. I had quit making films, so I had no need to be in Los Angeles. I returned home, to Memphis. I asked my father if he would sell me my foster-mother's old home, and he did. My long-time friend Dee helped me move in. Dee and I grew very close over the next few years, and he became like my friend Irving back in L. A., someone who would be very truthful with me about the choices I was making in my life.

Moving back into my childhood home and reconnecting with Dee and with members of my family I felt a sense of a circle completing itself. It was good to be back.

It was around this time that I met my play-son, Dennis. We actually first met in Houston, Texas, which I had forgotten until he reminded me. But we met again back in Memphis and I thought he was just the cutest thing in the world. It was after that that we developed what has become a very close relationship. I call him my son though I didn't go through the court system to be his dad. It's more that I took it upon myself to develop a father-son relationship and be the guidance in his life. He's twenty-five years old.

I also look on Dennis's partner 'Chester' as my adopted kid. So when I talk about my play-sons I mean Dennis and Chester. They both work for the city and are very educated and very mature for their age. When I met Dennis, he and Chester had already been partners for about three years. Their relationship was very successful and they had built a home together from the ground up.

Dennis is my heart, and if anything were to happen to me he would share in my possessions. He's very protective of me. He wants to know who's coming into my life; they have to pass his evaluation. Often when I go on a trip he'll travel with me. He'll make sure I get enough rest, and he'll stop people bothering me. It was he and Chester who pulled that crazy guy with the knife off me that time in Atlanta I told you about.

I had a period around two years ago, when both Dee and Irving died, when I felt like I was losing all my close friends, but in the midst of it my son was always there for me, helping me through my grief.

He's still there for me now, and we spend a lot of time together, me, him, and his mate. We don't do that much; we just go out to brunch and do dinner at each other's homes. We're a little group, and all during the winter-time, because we don't do a lot of cooking in the summer, each of us will take it in turns to host a dinner, and we'll go to each other's homes in fellowship. Me and my other friends, we're of an age where we're less into the club scene. Even my sons, who are much younger, of course, only go to clubs occasionally.

It was Dennis and Chester who encouraged me to take up my studies again. Watching them studying for their masters' degrees I thought to myself, "If they can do all of that, for sure I can do all of that." Their example inspired me to go back to college. By the time this book is out I should have graduated with a degree in criminal justice. My plan then is to head on and work on my master's. After that I'd like to attend law school, and maybe become a real-estate lawyer, and perhaps teach part-time.

I chose law because I've always been interested in legal matters, from criminal to constitutional. I've followed the politics of law and watched debates on it. My favorite television station would be Court TV. I always loved shows like *The Case-Files Of Doctor Henry Lee* and *Body Of Evidence*. Studying law means I can use my mind—I can investigate; I can analyze; I can assess. It's both challenging and stimulating.

Before I turned to studying, however, I had to think about earning a living. I owned my own home, I had money put aside, and I knew that I could bring in a decent amount from making personal appearances at clubs and hosting events, but I also wanted some definite regular source of income. But doing what?

I was pumping iron at the gym one day when one of the guys asked me on account of my size if I'd be interested in working security for a huge new club called Club Census that was in the makings here in Memphis. He didn't know I was Bobby Blake, just that I was this big, strong guy.

I wasn't that bothered, so I said, "Oh, whatever. Yeah, why not, I guess," and he arranged for me to go and speak to one of the managers, which I did.

"Oh, you're Bobby Blake!" the manager said excitedly the minute I put my head round the door. "I've got the chance to meet the famous Bobby Blake!"

Oh, shit, I thought, doing my best to keep a friendly smile on my face as I extended my hand for him to shake. Is this gonna mess up my possibility of getting employment here? Because one, it was a straight club and two, everyone thinks porn stars are all unreliable flakes who are strung out on drugs.

But then it turned out that not only was the manager a fan of mine, the owner of the club had actually met me. He and his wife had met me at the Adult Video News Conference in Las Vegas. He had been there because he owned adult bookstores in Memphis, Nashville, and other cities. I didn't remember him or his wife because I was meeting so many people at the time, but he told me when I met him again that the first time we met he had been telling me how much he makes off me in his bookstores. And now he had bought this club for his son to run.

I was hired on the spot. I did some training, and since I had experience of managing staff from my fast-food days, they asked me to take on the task of being chief of security. We set a special salary, $1,500 a week, and I oversaw the security team. I had about twenty guys working for me. I trained them and I managed them. Because of the way I ran things there were very few fights in the club, but if fights did break out I would let my team handle it, and then if they couldn't, I would step in.

The managers put a lot of trust in me. I had the alarm system combination, the keys—I would open up the club. I created a citywide radio network, gave all the guards radios and had them take them home so it meant I could always reach them if I needed them. Or if the business manager, who worked there during the day, needed someone to come up there to the office and I wasn't available, one of my staff could be called.

I worked for Club Census for around two years. It was a huge, upscale, state-of-the-art night-club, beautifully designed and award-winning. It had eight different bars and was one of America's top clubs, and even had—and still has—its own website, Censusthenightclub.com. The wealthy from all walks of life would be there, from drug-dealers to movie stars to legitimate business people. We had a lot of sports stars—football players, basketball players from the Memphis Grizzlies—and I looked out for them and made sure they were put in the VIP area. I treated my customers right.

Treating people right means you often get something in return. For instance, there's a guy here in Memphis who owns a hotel, and when he came to the club I always made sure he was well taken care of.

Now, sometimes when you meet someone you don't necessarily want to take them back to your own home and for whatever reason you can't, or don't want to, go back to their place. But you still want to fuck them. And when that was the case I would go to the owner's hotel and he would always give me a room for free.

"Bobby Blake is chief of security at Census!"
"A porn star is running security at Census!"
It was the subject of about a thousand blogs, and I was the talk of the town. Guys I was sure were straight would hit on me. Guys with gorgeous wives would want me to fuck them. And I did, and it was all good. It was astounding to me how many people recognized me on the door, not just guys on the Down Low, but straight people as well. And both men and women would hit me up online and say, "Oh, I just saw you at the club, you were wearing such-and-such suit, you looked so damn good I wanted to just eat you up!"

Shit just got so crazy. One time this guy invited me to his hotel room to fuck this chick. I went over there and he had this girl lying on the bed blindfolded. I recognized her—she was his wife. But I didn't let on, and we just took turns fucking her and everything. It was his fantasy, and hers as well.

A film was shot at Club Census called *Forty Shades of Blue*. I played the bouncer in that movie. It was a real good experience working with some of the people on that movie.

When it came out people called me and said, "Oh, I see you've gone mainstream now! Congratulations!"

So I had a lot of fun at Club Census. I enjoyed the work and people found favor in me. But after two years it came time for me to study full-time, so I decided to let the security work go. I'm still good friends with the owner, and have great memories of my time there.

Just last year my life took an unexpected turn when I was invited to perform a rap on a track by the out gay New York hip-hop artist Truedog. I know him because Truedog is originally from Memphis, and around twenty-five years ago we dated for a few. He was a dancer then, with big legs, a lovely ass, and a body to die for. Twenty years ago he moved to New York and we lost touch. I would often wonder how he was doing and one day, totally out of the blue, while I was online he hit me up.

We started talking and he asked me would I be interested in performing on a project he was working on, a hip-hop CD single for his label, Truedogrecords. I *was* interested, but had to admit that I wasn't big on singing. He said we could work round that, so I flew up to New York, we went into the studio, and I had a great time. It's amazing how good a studio can make you sound! It must have taken around six hours to lay down my part of the track, but Truedog boosted my confidence, made me feel good about myself, and made it easy.

Although I've never been a hip-hop fan I did it because I wanted to try something new. When we were first discussing the project Truedog said to me, "You're not going to have your way like you're used to having."

And I came back at him saying, "Get used to it. It has to be my way or I won't put my heart or voice or face to it."

He laughed and I laughed and we ended up working well together. Truedog's a down-to-earth brother who loves people and is a good person at heart. Once we'd done recording we talked about the old days and I came to find out that he had lied to me about his age back when we first met, and was actually younger than he had made out then. I asked him, "Why did you tell me you were nineteen?"

"Because I wanted to be with you," he said. "And that was all that mattered to me. I thought if I told you my right age you wouldn't be interested in me, you'd think I was just a kid."

Maybe he was right. In any case it was more of a friendship thing than a relationship between us.

By the time you're reading this book we should have shot the video for the track, and the single should be available to buy. It's called "Booty Ain't Got No Face," and the lyrics Truedog wrote that I performed run:

> *Sorry boy you ain't no fool*
> *I know they taught you that punk-ass crap at school*
> *You can go with a girl, you can mess with a dude*
> *Whatever happened is between him, her, and you*
> *You juvenile delinquent*
> *You better act like you know*
> *Booty ain't got no face. . .*

Now that I'm no longer working as a bouncer or filming porn my usual routine is: I wake up early in the morning, three-thirty to four a.m., check my emails, say my prayers, prepare myself for the gym, go to the gym, train some people and work out. Then I go to class, after which I go to the office. If I have a counseling session to do, I do it. Sometimes I have church meetings to attend. Mostly I spend time with my family, my son. Sometimes we go out to dinner or movies. We both enjoy going to the wrestling. My favorite wrestler's still The Rock, though he doesn't wrestle much anymore. In my church I'm an assistant—I'm director of the outreach department and do counseling work with young adults. Everyone there knows about me, and that I'm gay or bisexual. As always the way I carry myself means it's not a problem for me. If you know what you're talking about and you can speak with authority and you can walk with authority then that doesn't leave much room for doubt or questioning by those inclined to criticize—which is why I always prepare myself. Because if you're unprepared you're leaving space for a lot of questioning.

Now that I'm out of the world of adult films you might ask, would I want to be a pastor again? And my answer would be, no, not any more—that wore me out for a year and a half back at Greater Mount Pleasant and I wouldn't want it again. It's not my calling.

Now that I'm back in the church I counsel people from all

walks of life who are struggling with their sexual preferences. People who marry because they don't want that tag on them of being gay. People who live miserable lives because a pastor or preacher told them they were going to hell because of who or what they are.

I tell these troubled souls they don't belong to the pastor, to the bishop, or to the elders; they belong to God and God loves them whatever their sexuality. That none of us can mold anything; God is the potter and He does the molding. We can instill values in each other but at the close of the day God is the one who takes what we try to do and molds it not into what we want it to be, but what He wants it to be. I tell them that even though if I had the choice I wouldn't do it again, this is why I am not ashamed of my life—because what I did was what God had planned for me. And I tell them to pray and seek a close personal relationship with God and come to their own truth about their life, their sexuality.

I don't try and impose my own agenda on those I counsel. For instance, I recently spoke with a young gay man in Miami who said, "I wasn't born this way; I chose it." Now, my experience has been that my attraction to men has been there since I was a little boy; it's not a cup I went looking to drink from. So I tend to go along with and accept the fact that I was born this way. But I didn't argue with the young man who felt he chose his sexuality because it's not for me to impose my agenda on him. And perhaps for him it was true. In any case my advice to him was to strive to develop a personal relationship with God, and make sure that that relationship is a truthful one, and so find his own way in life.

I also became involved with an organization in Memphis called Friends for Life, an HIV-AIDS charity. During the course of my adventures as a porn star I would try to raise money for the cause of HIV awareness through doing workshops and guest appearances. Because of the nature of the adult business there was always some support for doing HIV-related charity work or giving money. And I had always been involved with outreach work supporting those living with AIDS, first off as an assistant chaplain in the Regional Medical Center in Memphis, then in Oakland, California with the Brother to Brother program.

A friend of mine, Anthony, was running a support group as part of Friends for Life called The Haven. He came to me and said, "Bobby, you have a great following, and the young people look up to you. I want you to be a part of this organization."

I was honored because I knew Anthony was a very hard worker, very dedicated and unafraid. He would hand out free condoms even when it wasn't popular with the African-American community to do so; people would walk by him out of fear of just being seen to take condoms. But he never gave up, and I applaud him for that. He did a great work, I would say a great ministry, and ran a very effective outreach department.

People would meet at The Haven and open their hearts on whatever was troubling them, from HIV-AIDS worries through family problems to issues of peer pressure, and would offer each other support.

I went to one of the group sessions and saw that some

young people do look up to me, and when I realized that I felt a great responsibility towards them. There were some young people who had dropped out of school, and we would raise money to ensure they could get back into school, making sure they had basic stuff like tennis shoes and school materials.

At one time I did sub-contracting work for Friends for Life and did group sessions and one-to-one counseling and outreach. I would tell young people they don't need to be effeminate just because they're gay. I would tell them the facts about HIV and that they should avoid these bareback parties that are happening all over the place. I would tell them that the new drugs aren't a magical cure, and that with the knowledge we have today there's no reason for somebody sixteen, seventeen years old to be HIV+, not catching it through sex, anyway. I'm upfront about the one bareback movie I made, and that I regret it, and that you don't need to make the mistake I made in having unsafe sex that way.

Also, although it was performing in adult films that made me famous, I always advise young gay men not to become involved in pornography. Porn is something you do because you feel in some way outcast from society, it seems to me. Perhaps there are other reasons, but I think for most of those involved in the adult industry it's the case. I stress that gay men don't need to be outcasts; they don't need to adopt an effeminate style, for which they will be derided. They don't need to drop out of school and get swallowed up by the gay scene and just club, club, club. They don't need to live in the fast lane sexually, because as I know all too well it's living in the fast lane that makes crossing over into porn so easy.

Even today I appreciate the opportunity Anthony gave me at The Haven to work more in depth with young people and be able to touch so many lives in a positive way, and bring about positive changes in others. I've always wanted to give back to society, and that has been a way of doing so.

On a smaller level I've donated art that people have sent me, portraits of myself and such, for The Haven to auction to raise funds for HIV awareness. Two years ago I donated my leather skirt to an international leather contest in Dallas for an HIV-AIDS fundraiser they were doing. So I'm very much involved in small ways in raising money for worthy causes. I was also part of World African-American HIV and AIDS Day, which happens each February, and the first year we did it we got a legendary gospel recording artist to donate his time. I won't name him as he did it for the cause and not the glory, but he played to a sell-out crowd and we raised a lot of money that day.

I still travel. I don't dance, but I do a lot of workshop guest appearances. I speak at seminars. On a lighter note I host fun events, too. Wet, the lube company, recently sponsored a wrestling match where the ring was full of Wet lube, and the guys wrestled in it. So that was a nice break from my more serious work.

One of the workshops I was invited to attend turned out to be a ticking time-bomb. Two years after I did it it was to blow up into a controversy that made the national news.

CHAPTER THIRTY-ONE:

CONTROVERSY

This whole thing blew up out of a workshop appearance I was invited to do in St. Louis, Missouri, by BABAA (Blacks Assisting Blacks Against Aids) which was then St. Louis' most prominent black AIDS service organization. The purpose of the workshop was to promote condom use among young black men who have sex with men, who are statistically the most at risk of any social group of becoming HIV+. This was back in 2002, and was around the time when pressure was starting to grow on educators to teach abstinence rather than safer sex techniques in order to receive federal monies for health education.

It's well-known that, for a number of reasons, young black gay men are a difficult group to reach when distributing safer sex and HIV-related information. Erise Williams, the head of BABAA, believed and believes in taking non-traditional approaches to get their attention. One year he organized a B-Boy Blues event, centering around the work of popular black gay author James Earl Hardy, and one year he invited me. I was booked to appear at an awareness-raising house party in July of 2002.

We agreed a booking fee of $500 and I went down there and did my appearance. As I was there as Bobby Blake the Porn Star I went bare-chested and wore boots and a towel, under which I had on shorts. I didn't dance or perform, I was just there to add glamour to the event.

Erise and I walked around with a basket in which were a lot of questions written on slips of paper about safe-sex related subjects. People would pull these questions out of the basket and see if they knew the answers, and we would educate on HIV and AIDS. So the idea was that having Bobby Blake the porn star there would get some young black gay men out of the house to see him, and they would end up learning something about HIV in a fun, informal environment.

Zero controversy, you may be thinking. I did the appearance, it went well, and I thought it was a successful event overall. I went home and thought no more about it.

Three months later the bomb went off when a guy named Kevin Coleman, who turned out to be BABAA's youth center director, and another employee got fired from the organization.

At that point this Kevin Coleman came up with an accusation that I had stripped, given lap-dances, and been nude when there were kids around. Apparently—according to him—there was also meant to have been a female stripper there, but I certainly never saw any such person, so I don't know where that came from.

Of course it bothered me when I eventually heard about

it a few weeks later, because first off there were no kids there, and second, Erise had invited me because he knew I did workshops and seminars that reached people effectively, not because he wanted a stripper to perform. The issue of me being sexual around under-age youngsters, never mind kids, particularly angered me because I've always been especially condemnatory of gay clubs whose managements are slack about checking that the young gay men coming through their doors are of a proper age to be there. Gay teens need protecting from an environment that can be harmful if you lack the maturity to deal with it, and I feel that club owners, who after all are making money off the backs of gay men, have a moral duty of care towards them. All too often, though, it's just about the dollars, and that saddens and angers me.

Anyway, apparently Kevin Coleman, who is supposedly heterosexual, had photographs he'd taken at the event that he showed to the *St. Louis Post Dispatch* and local TV stations, and they took up the story and blew it up into a scandal.

The accusations came to nothing of course, because they were untrue, but in the meantime all sorts of trouble had been made. To my mind hiring me to do an appearance was perfectly legitimate, but when you take federal money then how you spend it is often extremely circumscribed. The City of St. Louis Department of Health began invest-igating Coleman's complaint on behalf of the Center for Disease Control. Nothing in my conduct could be proved to be inappropriate, as Coleman had alleged, but the CDC got mad that I had been paid out of a $96,000 grant that had been ear-marked to fight syphilis. As a result, Erise and Senior Director James Green were fired from BABAA.

Erise said in an interview I read, "It was like a part of my life being sucked out of me because I had, some time ago, decided to dedicate my life to it." He had made BABAA his life mission, leading it for most of its thirteen years, and is widely credited with having turned it from a small outfit into a $1.2 million, 28-staffer agency. He said he and James Green were fired because the Republican administration could make political hay from the scandal and would use it to undermine funding of all AIDS Service Organizations. "We were the fall guys," Erise said.

BABAA's board vice-chair Donnell Smith didn't disagree, saying he was told that the scandal meant that unless Erise and James Green left BABAA's funding would be terminated.

Erise didn't apologize for his approach to outreach work, despite being fired for it. But that's what you get if your organization gets all of its funding from the CDC, which is a rigid, controlling government body with a fixed way of doing things.

For myself, I was mad because this white female investigator from the CDC never asked anybody any questions. She never spoke to me or, as far as I know, anyone else who was at the actual event; she just jumped to conclusions, and what was left of the grant got pulled.

Meanwhile things got messier and messier, with suits and counter-suits. James Green sued BABAA for unpaid sick and holiday pay. Kevin Coleman planned to sue for sexual harassment he claimed to have experienced from colleagues who repeatedly insinuated he was gay while he ran the youth center—but then let it be known he would drop the charges if he was reinstated in his post. What was that all about?

And all this time my name was on the wings of the morning, my picture was on the television, a lot of people's pictures were on TV, and I was frustrated because what amounted to unsubstantiated charges were being made against me in a public forum. But when I went to sue—I heard Kevin Coleman and James Green got paid—I was told there was no more money left. So I let it go. But it was angering to be lied on. It was also angering to have these accusations made against me be reported on, and then, when they came to nothing, nobody in the media ever troubled to point out that they were, in fact, a bunch of lies served up by a bitter ex-employee.

My faith in God helped keep me strong in that difficult time. I would brace myself up and remind myself, "Everything that happens is part of His plan."

And on an earthly level my friend Anthony from The Haven told me, "Bobby, keep going. The gay black kids need you. They look up to you."

That gave me heart, and he and the other men and women who came to The Haven to talk about whatever was on our minds, and offer each other comfort and support, were my rock in a hard time.

But still I felt trapped; you can't control the media. You can't control television.

It was then that Keith Boykin came to my rescue. Keith is

a black gay activist who was an administrator in the Clinton administration, and both in his website and on his show on Black Entertainment Television he spoke up for me, saying it made perfect sense for someone who had worked in the sex industry to promote sexual health and HIV-related issues, and that my presence at the event made sense as the chance to meet a porn star would have encouraged younger, less generally aware black gay men to attend and learn about safer sex practices. Keith has a following all over the world, and after he had spoken up for me I got calls from magazines, from newspaper people, and even from television people wanting to hear my side of the story. Wanting to hear the truth. It was a massive relief.

As far as BABAA goes, well, you reap what you sow. A tree is known by the fruit it bears and I've never seen an apple tree produce pears. I hear they lost a lot of their funding. They changed their name to REACH St. Louis, but from what I hear the director's hours have been cut and they're pretty much closing down. And God elevated Erise Williams; he started a new agency called Williams & Associates, and I understand they're doing good work on HIV-AIDS issues in the St. Louis area. The guy who lied, Kevin Coleman, has since left the area, I hear.

It seems sad to me that someone would lie on other people, try to destroy them, and in the process stop a lot of good work from being done.

It was a difficult time for me, but nothing that happened then deterred me from trying to make a positive difference in people's lives, and that's something I continue to do to this day. God saw fit for me to be tested and it made me a stronger person, and all the more determined to continue educating people of all colors about safe sex.

CHAPTER THIRTY-TWO:

STATE OF
THE NATION

In my time I've traveled all over the country, I've lived in a number of cities, and I've observed certain things that have stuck with me. In this chapter I'd like to share a few of those things.

One is we still have a big North-South divide. In the South people are more conservative and there's more of a sense of the family unit, even amongst gay folks. People in the South are more friendly, more caring, more sharing. Take myself—even though I never touch alcohol I have a bar in my home. I have shelves of liquor and I keep coolers of wine even though neither I nor my parents ever drank. When I did my guest room I put a nice big bed in there, and satellite, and a computer. I tried to look out for my guests like I look out for myself, and that's very much a Southern thing.

Having said that, when I lived in Atlanta, which is a Southern city, I found the men very whorish; relationships were very free and easy there, and infidelity was common-place. There were very few monogamous relationships. I found this also to be true of Washington, D. C. and New York. I always remember how, when I danced in those cities, I would meet couples, and then the next day one or other half of the couple would turn up again, and come on to me behind his mate's back.

Up north there's a mixture of attitudes; they're more friendly on the East coast, I would say. On the West coast there's a lot of folks with their heads stuck up they ass. In Los Angeles everyone pretends like they've got so much—they're just a bunch of stuck-up-ass people to me. And here's some-thing I've run into time and again, which I can't stand—black men who put out that they only date white men, and white men who put out that they only date black men. I have a problem with that. People have preferences, I'm sure. But what it says to me is something's wrong with my own—I'm off-limits to my own. What's wrong with your own? There are some folks who wish they were black, some folks wish they were white. Why? It's only skin color and hair texture. If someone white comes up to me and says, "I only date black guys," then I'll say to him he lost me right there.

I find men of all races attractive, and I date men of all races—black, white, Latino, Asian—I date across the board. I've had a white lover, 'Gary'. Beautiful, blond, and from Connecticut. We had some good times together, walking on the beach and being romantic and such, but after about a year he said, "Bobby, I can't take the pressure." He couldn't deal with my fame; it wasn't a racial thing.

When I went to The Hustlers' Ball in Berlin in Germany around three years ago I met a gorgeous white boy named Steven with the body of a Greek god. We shared a beautiful experience and I'm still in touch with him.

What's more important to me than a person's race is that there's no bullshit; that there's no lying, no game-playing, and no dirt or slovenliness. I have zero tolerance for filth or any of the rest of it. I date, but I'm very happy not being in a relationship right now.

The Hustlers' Ball was an experience in itself. I was invited by Rentaboys Productions to be their special guest. Lots of people turned out to see me, so many they were turning them away at the door. I met people from all over the world. I met the Boys of Budapest. I actually put on a show—I fucked three or four guys on stage and the crowd went wild; they loved it. It was fun, and at the end of it I met Steven.

I also learned that American money is shit. What it costs to live like a king or a queen in New York is only enough to keep you struggling by in Germany.

When it comes to race I've never had any problems; I love everybody and don't get into hating. I try to treat others the way I want to be treated. Racism is alive and well, unfortunately, but I don't think you should let it control your life. You shouldn't say that you're unable to do this or that, or fulfill your dream because of racism. We have to move away from that mindset because it's like a virus and it destroys us.

Speaking of racism, when I was living in Florida with Flex I became very aware of Miami as a nice place to visit but a bad place to live if you're black. Being a corrections officer, which was something Flex had done before I met him, is considered a good job if you're black in South Florida. If they wanted to enjoy themselves black gay people would have to go and try and mix in with the other races at Club Twist on South Beach because the only black gay club, Sugar's, which was white-owned, was a hole in the ground. It was just a box, and it was in the worst part of town, the area where you were most likely to get robbed or get your car stolen. At that time there were no black-owned black clubs, only a few promoters renting out space. Club Boy was an example of that, and that was held in a bad part of town, too.

Other cities I felt had more of a problem with racism than average were St. Louis, Dallas, and New Orleans, and South Carolina in general.

It was when I was living in Florida that I became aware of the very different way refugees were treated when they washed up on America's shores. Cubans, if they reached land, were welcomed. Haitians were thrown back. It was the law but it was nothing but naked racism.

I have to say that, although things are getting a little better with the younger people, there's still racism in the gay community, and that's one reason why I've resisted endorsing gay agendas, concepts, and theories. They want me to endorse their policies when they don't want me to join their country clubs. They get mad at the heterosexual community for being prejudiced against them, but then they won't let their other gay brothers and sisters be part of their organizations. And what is that if not prejudice?

One agenda I do endorse, though, is affirmative action. It

levels the field, not just for the African-American community, but for minorities in general. I think it's still needed
because we continue to live in an unjust, unfair United States
of America. Women are overlooked. As I've said, Cubans
who make it here illegally are allowed to stay, but Haitians
are sent back. Now, whatever you think about illegal immigrants, and I do think we need to protect our borders
because their presence depresses wages and makes it hard for
poorer people here to feed their families, policies towards
illegal immigrants should be fair and just. I have a problem
with the "Land of the Free and Home of the Brave" using
racial profiling in deciding who should be thrown back and
who let in.

I was impressed by the Million Man March, especially the
second one, when they included everybody, gays and all. It
takes time for doors to open. Even the doors in your house;
you've got the key and it still takes time to open them, and
some of these doors have been closed for a very long time. As
far as Farrakhan goes, you have to know what to take in and
what not to take in. We don't like to deal with reality, and
what he often does is raise issues that we would prefer to
sweep under the carpet, whether we agree with his conclusions and solutions or not. In any event it was well-planned,
and I had the opportunity to meet a lot of brothers, open-
minded brothers from across the country. They weren't all
gay, just open-minded. It was a unique event, and I enjoyed
it.

I've always been interested in politics and very engaged
with current affairs. I can sit down with anyone and talk

about politics as far back in the day as Anwar Sadat, Menachin Begin, Egypt, and Israel. I look at the situation with Israel and the Lebanese today and I think it's a tragedy. I have some problems with how Israel handled the situation. I know they're tired of Hezbollah shooting rockets into their territory and making things uncomfortable, but still was it right for them to destroy all those peoples' homes while proclaiming they were hide-outs for Hezbollah? So many innocent people were killed, and yet there Hezbollah still is. And at the conclusion of the whole matter what amazed me was that Hezbollah gave each of those households that were destroyed $12,000.

Compare that with the situation in New Orleans, after Hurricane Katrina—what did the individual devastated households there receive? A good many of them got nothing at all. So here's Hezbollah, called by our government a terrorist arm, helping their people in a straightforward and concrete fashion while our government does little or nothing to help the poor of New Orleans. This administration is horrible.

This current administration is the worst we've ever had. Our current president is worse even than his father. He didn't get into office in the right manner, and this Iraq war is a personal agenda of his. We've been lied to over and over. Bush declared victory, and since then thousands of our soldiers and many more thousands of innocent bystanders in Iraq have been killed. Bush plays mind games with war and leads people to fear we'll be attacked, and that negotiation is a sign of weakness. But sometimes it's good to talk, to come to an understanding. Even in the Bible it says, "Come now and let us reason together." And you have to reason, you have to negotiate, because we can't police the entire world. We've gone to Iraq and tried to make Iraq a country like our country. But you can't force democracy onto a country like that. So my perspective is this administration is the worst I've ever witnessed or even read about in history books.

So I don't admire Bush. I did admire Bill Clinton, and how up under pressure he was able to continue to keep our country going in the right direction. I feel he loved people across the board and whole-heartedly.

I don't say that just because he had a good reputation with the African-American community. When he was in office I made as much money as I did because the economy was doing well, and because the adult business always prospers under the Democrats. The Republicans are anti-porn and tend to be repressive towards the industry.

I also admire Hillary Clinton. And I loved Margaret Thatcher, who I followed for years. She was one of the longest-running prime ministers of England. She ruled with an iron fist, they say, but to me I loved her because she showed the world that there are some females who are capable of running a government and doing so effectively.

When I was in eleventh and twelfth grade I was a part of the Shelby County Democratic Executive Board in Memphis. It taught me to study each individual candidate's record, and not just vote on whether they're Republican or Democrat or Independent.

Back in those days I ran for state representative. I just

wanted to throw my name in the ring and run and have that experience. This was before I was even involved in porn.

Soon enough I had all these news people calling me. And they started asking me all these wild questions, intrusive personal questions, and I just thought, "Hell, no, this is too much." It was like they went back to the day before I was *born*. It was madness, and I quickly withdrew from the race. But I continued to follow politics keenly, and I still do today.

CHAPTER THIRTY-THREE:

WHY?

On television just recently there was a special about HIV and AIDS and how it has taken hold in the African-American community, and how so many pastors and churches have turned their backs on the issue until now; infection rates are at epidemic levels. One bisexual man who appeared on the program was married and had just buried his wife. They were both HIV+, but she was in denial about it and refused to take her medication, and so she died. He and others talked about how someone having HIV was considered a hush-hush thing in the family, something to not be addressed. But the time has come for one of the most powerful backbones of the African-American community to address it: the Black Church.

Unfortunately I do feel that the Black Church has become somewhat of a social club for those who have to the exclusion of the have-nots. If you don't put a lot of money on the plate most pastors won't want to know you, and if you pass away they won't preach your funeral but will send the associate minister instead. There is an element of hypocrisy, as if everyone doesn't have some sort of skeleton in his or her closet, and an excess of claiming to be better than other people, and putting other people down.

Also, going to a lot of churches you hear preachers get up and throw words of condemnation on homosexuality as if it's the only sin. Now, even if you consider that homo-sexuality is a sin, why obsess on it? What about all the other sins that have much more of a real impact on people's lives? What use is all that condemnation? They mix homosexuality up with child-molesting, which is just plain incorrect, and a slander on gay men. They used to say that AIDS was God's punishment for homosexuality. Remember that? Now that the majority of people living with HIV-AIDS are heterosexual black Africans they've had to stop saying that. But those very same preachers don't say, "Well, I was wrong on that, I need to rethink my attitude." They just keep acting like they never said it and the judgmental attitude remains.

I feel there is a need to preach the whole gospel. In other words, tell me what I am doing wrong, show me the right way, teach me, correct me, don't just throw me away. And the Black Church has thrown so many people away.

The whole phenomenon of the Down Low, which I would say is just bisexuality in the main, is a product of this judgmental attitude. If you feel an outcast, if you feel condemned, then you won't open up and be honest about yourself. You will conceal your true nature. People want to feel welcome. They want to feel cared for, even in their weakest moments. Especially in their weakest moments. So this

Down Low situation, where the women blame the men for not opening up to them, is a case of asking the wrong question. The women must take responsibility for themselves and understand that the men are stifled by the attitude of the Church. The Church doesn't have to approve of homosexuality or bisexuality. I don't ask for that acceptance. But it needs to put condemnation aside and try to make people comfortable. Nobody wants to be disrespected. Nobody wants to be looked down on or stepped on. It was that judgmental attitude that made me so angry and frustrated that I left the Church in the first place. It was that condemnatory mentality that sent me out into the world of adult porn to do the things I've done. I was made to feel an outcast, and I did things that, had I been accepted as who I truly was by the Church, had I not felt rejected on account of my sexuality, I would never have done. It's for that reason I say that, though I'm not ashamed of what I've done, I do regret it. Because what felt like a free choice at the time I made it was in truth one that was pushed upon me by a Church and by a society at large that wouldn't accept me for who I was.

Now that it's over I can accept that that journey was all part of God's plan for me. And now I have made that journey I can see that I have a certain task before me—to be an educator. To help educate others when so many in the African-American community are still so ignorant about HIV and AIDS. As the Bible says, it is because of a lack of knowledge that men perish. I want to try and instill positive values. I want to counsel those despairing over their sexuality to the point of suicide and make them see that their lives are not worthless, and tell them their lifestyle isn't sending them to Hell. I want to encourage the church to step up to the plate and deal with the HIV epidemic that has invaded our community. I want to make a difference in our community, to restore hope to the hopeless. I want to be a part of doing positive things that will make a difference not just in our community, but world-wide.

It is enough.

THE END.